WILD BIRD GUIDES

Eastern Bluebird

WILD BIRD GUIDES

Eastern Bluebird

Gary Ritchison

STACKPOLE BOOKS

For Tameria Dawn, Brandon Tyler,
and Brianna Carol

Published by
STACKPOLE BOOKS
5067 Ritter Road
Mechanicsburg, PA 17055
www.stackpolebooks.com

Printed in China

10 9 8 7 6 5 4 3 2 1

First edition

Cover photo by Bill Leaman

Cover design by Tracy Patterson

Library of Congress Cataloging-in-Publication Data

Ritchison, Gary.
    Eastern bluebird / Gary Ritchison. — 1st ed.
      p.   cm. — (Wild bird guides)
    Includes bibliographical references.
    ISBN 0-8117-2745-9 (pb)
    1. Eastern bluebird. I. Title. II. Series.
QL696.P288 R57   2000   99-047530
598.8′42—dc21   CIP

Contents

Acknowledgments

Thanks to Bret Huntsman for working with me to learn more about Eastern Bluebirds. Financial support for our study of bluebird singing behavior was provided by the North American Bluebird Society and the Department of Biological Sciences at Eastern Kentucky University. Thanks also to Barbara Rupard and Jackie King for superior secretarial assistance, to T. D. Pitts for providing a copy of his dissertation, to Linda Peterson Janilla for permission to include her recipe for Bluebird Banquet, and to Dorene H. Scriven and Myrna Pearman for their many helpful comments on the manuscript. Much of what we know about Eastern Bluebirds—and much of the information in this book—has been reported in the many excellent publications of Patricia Adair Gowaty and her colleagues, David C. Krieg, Benedict C. Pinkowski, T. David Pitts, and Lawrence Zeleny. Thanks to them, and to many others listed in the References section of this book, for their efforts to better understand Eastern Bluebirds. Finally, I thank my beautiful wife, Tameria Dawn; my terrific son, Brandon Tyler; and my equally terrific daughter, Brianna Carol, for sharing my love of nature and for continuing to make our "nest" in Hilltop Acres a most delightful home.

An Introduction

"The bluebird is like a speck of clear blue sky seen near the end of a storm, reminding us of an ethereal region and a heaven which we had forgotten. His soft warble melts in the ear, as the snow is melting in the valleys around. The bluebird comes and with his warble drills the ice and sets free the rivers and ponds and frozen ground." So wrote Henry David Thoreau in 1859 concerning the spring arrival of Eastern Bluebirds after a long Concord winter.

John Burroughs, a naturalist and writer of the late nineteenth and early twentieth centuries, wrote, "The first bluebird in the spring is as welcome as the blue sky itself. The season seems softened and tempered as soon as we hear his note and see his warm breast and azure wing." With the formation of a national organization with thousands of members who care about bluebirds and the hard work of many to provide nest sites for these birds, it's obvious that these sentiments are shared by many people.

The Eastern Bluebird was formally described by the Swedish biologist Carolus Linnaeus in 1758 and given the scientific name *Motacilla sialis*. Linnaeus placed Eastern Bluebirds in the genus *Motacilla* because he suspected a close relationship to other birds in that genus, the wagtails. The specific name *sialis* is of Greek origin and, in the writings (actually a recipe book) of the second-century author Athenaeus, refers to an unknown species of bird. William Swainson, an English naturalist and artist, realized that Eastern Bluebirds were not that closely related to wagtails and in 1827 created a new genus for the three bluebird species, simply changing the last letter of the word *sialis*. Since then, the scientific name for the Eastern Bluebird has been *Sialia sialis*.

Over the years, Eastern Bluebirds have had a variety of common names, including Blue Robin, Blue Redbreast, American Bluebird, and Red-breasted Bluebird. Many people, including John James Audubon, have simply called them bluebirds. Eastern Bluebird is most appropriate, however, because the species occurs primarily in the eastern United States, and its range largely occurs east of those of the Western and Mountain Bluebirds.

Adult Eastern Bluebirds are about 6 to 8 inches (16 to 21 centimeters) long and weigh about 1.1 ounces (30 grams), with no significant difference in size between male and female. The sexes do, however, differ in appearance. Males have bright blue upperparts, a rusty or reddish orange throat and breast, and a white belly. Females are blue-gray above, with dull blue wings and tail. The throat and breast are a more subdued reddish orange. Both males and females have short black bills that are slightly notched at the tip and black legs and feet.

Recently fledged bluebirds are brownish above with white or buffy spots and streaks below. The wings and tails of young bluebirds are blue, with differences between the brighter blue males and duller blue females apparent as early as twelve days after hatching. The spots and streaks in the plumage of young bluebirds are typical of all young and some adults in the thrush family, of which the bluebirds are members. Young bluebirds spend much of their time perched in the dense foliage of trees, especially during the first several days after fledging, and their plumage provides excellent camouflage.

Eastern Bluebirds vary slightly in size and appearance throughout their broad range. In Arizona and northern Mexico, they are a bit larger and paler than those in the eastern United States, and Florida birds have slightly longer bills than those farther north.

Species in which males and females differ in coloration, such as Eastern Bluebirds, are called dichromatic. Female Eastern Bluebirds have relatively dull plumage; such plumage may reduce visibility and the chances of being spotted by a predator. Although the bright coloration of the males presumably makes them easier for predators to spot, it provides them with important advantages. th the bright blue above and the reddish ge of the throat and breast likely aid in interactions with other Eastern ds.

Correlations between plumage color or quality and male behavior and status have been reported in several species of birds. For example, female European Kestrels prefer males with brighter plumage (bluer tails and redder backs) and for good reason. Observations revealed that brighter males spent more time hunting than duller males, and females mated with bright males produced more offspring than those mated with dull males. Although there have been no such studies of Eastern Bluebirds, males with brighter upperparts and breasts may be more attractive to females and may do better in interactions with other males.

Male and female bluebirds get their reddish breast coloration from pigments called carotenoids present in some of the foods they eat. Ingested carotenoids are deposited in feathers during molt, when the new feathers are developing, and the amount of carotenoids ingested influences plumage coloration. So the quality of a male bluebird's red plumage is linked to the quality of his diet, and diet in turn is influenced by a male's foraging skills, coordination, and vision. Thus it seems likely that a better-quality male would have a better-quality diet and therefore a brighter, redder breast.

To a human observer, the bright blue plumage of a male bluebird would seem to be a more obvious advertisement of quality than the reddish orange breast. Blue plumage, however, is not caused by pigments deposited in the feathers. The bluebird's blue body, wing, and tail feathers are contour feathers, and such feathers have a stiff shaft, or rachis, plus numerous barbs that extend from the shaft to create the broad, flat vanes on either side. The top of each barb has a thin layer of transparent cells, each of which contains numerous tiny particles. When sunlight hits those particles, the short, blue wavelengths are scattered, while the other wavelengths are absorbed. As a result, we—and other bluebirds—see bright blue feathers.

Recent studies of Blue Grosbeaks, another species with a lot of blue plumage, have revealed differences among males in the hue and intensity of their blue plumage that are not obvious to the human eye. Our eyes allow us to see blue and violet light—light with wavelengths as short as about 400 nanometers. The eyes of songbirds, in contrast, can see light with wavelengths as short as 370 nanometers—what we call ultraviolet light. The blue plumage of male Blue Grosbeaks, when viewed at these shorter wavelengths, exhibits much individual variation. This variation appears to be correlated with differences in male quality: male Blue Grosbeaks that ate better during molt had bluer feathers. Further, female Blue Grosbeaks that paired with bluer males tended to lay more eggs. Thus bluer plumage seems to indicate higher-quality males, and females benefit by pairing with such males. This is likely true for Eastern Bluebirds as well.

Although the plumage of female Eastern Bluebirds is more subdued, there is probably individual variation in plumage quality. Little is currently known about the possible relationship between female plumage and quality, but brighter plumage may indicate a better diet. Brighter females may be in better condition and therefore able to produce larger clutches.

Beyond attractive plumage, Eastern Bluebirds represent an important conservation story. Beginning in the late 1800s and continuing well into the twentieth century, Eastern Bluebird populations plummeted by as much as 90 percent. Several factors contributed to the decline of this cavity-nesting species; among the most important was the introduction into North America of two nest-site competitors, the House Sparrow and the European Starling.

During the late 1800s, an amateur ornithologist and Shakespeare aficionado named Eugene Schieffelin decided to introduce into the United States all birds referred to in the works of Shakespeare. One of those birds was the European Starling, pictured here, which spread slowly at first, but then rapidly expanded its range until it occupied most of the Eastern Bluebird's range. By the mid-1950s, the starling population in the United States was estimated at 50 million. The competition from this aggressive cavity nester limited the availability of suitable nest sites for Eastern Bluebirds and contributed to a decline in bluebird populations that lasted about one hundred years.

House Sparrows were first introduced to the United States in 1851 in a failed attempt to help control caterpillars in New York City. They spread rapidly and could be found throughout much of the Eastern Bluebird's range by the mid-1880s. The aggressive and increasingly numerous sparrows took over the cavities formerly used by bluebirds, and bluebirds began to disappear from cities, towns, and adjacent areas during the late 1800s.

But the Eastern Bluebird story has a happy ending. Populations stabilized by the mid- to late 1960s, and since 1980 they have generally increased. Several factors have contributed to this reversal, including the increased availability of nest sites, due to the efforts of untold numbers of bluebird enthusiasts, and declines in European Starling and, especially, House Sparrow populations, for reasons that are as yet unclear.

All this is good news for those who care about Eastern Bluebirds, and fortunately for bluebirds, the number of such folks continues to grow. Many of these enthusiasts know a lot about bluebirds; those just developing an interest in these fascinating birds may know very little. Over the past thirty years, detailed observations, experiments, and laboratory work have revealed much about the behavior and ecology of Eastern Bluebirds. This book is an attempt to share this information.

2

Taxonomy and Distribution

Bird species with broad geographic distributions, such as bluebirds, are commonly divided into subspecies, because groups of individuals separated for some time from other such groups often develop slightly different characteristics. Ornithologists designate subspecies by adding a third word after the genus and species. Eastern Bluebirds have been divided into eight subspecies: *Sialia sialis sialis* (eastern United States, southern Canada, and northeastern Mexico), *Sialia sialis bermudensis* (Bermuda), *Sialia sialis grata* (central and south Florida), *Sialia sialis nidificans* (east coast of Mexico), *Sialia sialis fulva* (Mexico and southern Arizona), *Sialia sialis guatemalae* (southern Mexico and Guatemala), *Sialia sialis meridionalis* (Honduras, northern El Salvador, and Nicaragua), and *Sialia sialis caribaea* (Nicaragua and eastern Honduras).

Size and plumage differences are minor, with overlap among subspecies. Most studies of Eastern Bluebirds have focused on the subspecies that occurs in the eastern United States, *S. s. sialis;* in general, the behavior and ecology of all of the subspecies are very similar.

The genus *Sialia* occurs only in North America and includes three species: Eastern Bluebirds, Western Bluebirds *(Sialia mexicana),* and Mountain Bluebirds *(Sialia currucoides).* Molecular analysis suggests that these three species began diverging from a common ancestral species about 2.5 million years ago. All male bluebirds are blue above. Male Eastern Bluebirds have a rusty throat and breast, male Western Bluebirds have a blue throat and rusty breast, and male Mountain Bluebirds have a blue throat and blue breast.

The females of all three species look similar, with some blue in the wings and tail. The plumage of female bluebirds is patterned after that of the males, though duller. Where males are blue, female bluebirds tend to be blue-gray or gray, and where males have deep rusty plumage, females have pale rusty or brownish gray plumage. Throat color can be useful for distinguishing female Eastern and Western bluebirds; that of female Eastern Bluebirds is usually lighter, whitish versus gray. The best field mark may be belly color: white in female Eastern Bluebirds and gray in Western. Posture can also be useful in identifying species. Female Mountain Bluebirds have longer wings and legs and a slimmer, less hunchbacked look than the other two species. In many areas of North America, the ranges of these three species do not overlap.

During the breeding season, Western Bluebirds can be found west of the Great Plains in the United States and southern British Columbia, and in western Mexico south to Puebla (just south of Mexico City), but they are most abundant in California, Arizona, and New Mexico. Most Western Bluebirds are resident, so their winter range is similar to their breeding range, although individuals that breed at higher elevations move to lower altitudes during the winter.

Mountain Bluebirds breed at high elevations throughout the western United States, western Canada, and southeastern Alaska. They are the most migratory of the three species, and most individuals that breed in Alaska and Canada move south for the winter. Those that breed in the northern United States move farther south or to lower altitudes. Most Mountain Bluebirds spend the winter in the southwestern United States, including southeastern Colorado, eastern New Mexico, southwestern Texas, and southern California. Many also winter in the open areas of southern Oregon, northern California, and northwestern Nevada. Individuals occasionally stray from normal migration routes; Mountain Bluebirds have been infrequently sighted as far from their normal range as Pennsylvania and New York.

Like other bluebirds, Mountain Bluebirds feed primarily on insects captured on the ground. When available, they use perches for hunting in the same manner as Eastern Bluebirds. When perches are not available, however, Mountain Bluebirds search for insects while hovering several feet above the ground. They are able to hover because they have longer wings and more surface area of wing relative to body weight than Eastern and Western Bluebirds. This ability to hover, and the reduced dependence on perches compared with Eastern and Western Bluebirds, enables Mountain Bluebirds to occupy areas with few trees and shrubs.

Eastern Bluebirds bear some resemblance to other, less closely related species. Male Blue Grosbeaks are about the same size as bluebirds but are chunkier in appearance and blue overall, having darker wings with rusty wing bars and conical bills. Male Indigo Buntings (shown here) are completely blue, with darker wings and tails, and are noticeably smaller than bluebirds. Female Blue Grosbeaks and Indigo Buntings are brown with light streaking, resembling sparrows and bearing no resemblance to female Eastern Bluebirds. The male Lazuli Bunting, a bird of the western United States, bears a stronger resemblance to the Eastern Bluebird, being blue above with rusty plumage on the breast and a white belly, but it has broad white wing bars and a blue throat and is noticeably smaller than the bluebird. Also, the ranges of the two birds are largely separate.

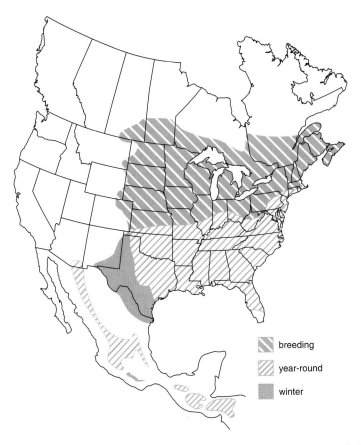

breeding

year-round

winter

Eastern Bluebirds occur east of the Rocky Mountains from southern Canada south to Honduras and El Salvador. There is also a resident population in Bermuda. Because bluebirds are partially migratory, the breeding range differs from the wintering range. The breeding range includes the eastern United States; southern Canada, from Nova Scotia west to southeastern Saskatchewan; parts of Mexico and Central America; and Bermuda. In the northern portion of their range, including New England and southern Canada, numbers of breeding bluebirds are generally low.

The western edge of the breeding range of Eastern Bluebirds extends south from southeastern Alberta along the western borders of North Dakota, South Dakota, Nebraska, Kansas, and Oklahoma through central Texas, although fewer breeding birds are found in western North and South Dakota, western Nebraska, western Kansas, and the Oklahoma panhandle. Eastern Bluebirds also breed in extreme southern Arizona and south into Mexico and Central America, including Guatemala, El Salvador, and Honduras.

During the fall and winter, Eastern Bluebirds leave the more northerly portions of their range. Typically, few wintering bluebirds are observed north of a line extending from Connecticut west through the northern sections of Pennsylvania, Ohio, Indiana, and Illinois and continuing through southern Iowa and Nebraska. Bluebirds that breed north of this line are largely migratory and move varying distances south for the winter. The tendency of bluebirds to migrate declines with decreasing latitude. In southern Illinois, slightly more than half of the resident bluebirds typically remain throughout the winter. South of North Carolina, Tennessee, northern Arkansas, and northern Oklahoma, most bluebirds are probably year-round residents. Although most Eastern Bluebirds winter within the species' breeding range, some do not, spending the winter in New Mexico, southeastern Arizona, or even Cuba.

Most Eastern Bluebirds winter in the southeastern United States, in the area between 30 degrees north latitude, from northern Florida west along the Gulf coasts of Alabama, Mississippi, Louisiana, and Texas, and 40 degrees north latitude, from Maryland west through the southern portions of Pennsylvania, Ohio, Indiana, Illinois, and extending through northern Missouri and northern Kansas. The western border of the primary wintering range of Eastern Bluebirds extends south from central Kansas through Oklahoma and central Texas.

The northern limit of the bluebird's wintering range is correlated with temperature.
Few bluebirds winter in areas where min-
imum temperatures consistently fall below
about 20 degrees F. Because few or no insects
are available during cold weather, bluebirds
depend on fruit. As long as fruit is available,
bluebirds can survive surprisingly low temperatures. But fruit supplies continue to
diminish during the winter, as other birds
and animals use the same resource. If supplies are depleted during a period of cold
weather, a bluebird may not be able to locate
another source and may not survive. Cold
weather during late winter and early spring
makes survival difficult for Eastern Bluebirds,
because food supplies may be depleted by
that time of year.

Historically, the western limit of the Eastern
Bluebird's wintering and breeding range has
been influenced by precipitation and, perhaps, the presence of Mountain and Western
Bluebirds. The western Great Plains region
receives too little precipitation to support
much woody vegetation, and Eastern Bluebirds need such vegetation for nesting and
foraging. In addition, the ranges of both
Western and Mountain Bluebirds border
or overlap the western limit of the Eastern
Bluebird's range. Similarities among these
species in foraging tactics and prey use may
create interspecific competition, limiting the
western range of Eastern Bluebirds.

During the late 1800s and early 1900s, Eastern Bluebirds expanded their range west into the Great Plains. As settlers moved into the plains, they planted trees and erected fences, which provided nest sites and hunting perches. More recent range expansion may also be the result of human activity. The cutting of forests in the Southwest plus grazing by cattle in areas that formerly had thicker undergrowth and dense foliage may have created open habitats suitable for Eastern Bluebirds.

In some areas, the breeding range of Eastern Bluebirds overlaps that of Western and Mountain Bluebirds. Because the three species require similar resources, they usually don't inhabit the same areas within the overlapped ranges. Where breeding ranges do overlap, Eastern and Mountain Bluebirds may compete for resources, but populations of both species are low in areas of overlap, which not only limits competition but occasionally leads to hybridization. Finding a mate may be difficult in areas with low numbers of bluebirds, and as a result, Eastern Bluebirds occasionally pair with Mountain Bluebirds. Because the two species are closely related, such pairs are as likely to produce young as intraspecific pairs. Such hybrids are able to breed successfully with either species.

Some bird species have very specific habitat requirements, others very general, and most somewhere in between. Breeding Bachman's Warblers (a species now thought to be extinct) required flooded swamp forests with extensive cane thickets. In contrast, Northern Cardinals can be found in a wide range of habitats, ranging from cities to deciduous forests to cypress swamps to pine plantations. The habitat requirements of Eastern Bluebirds are certainly not as restrictive as those of Bachman's Warblers and, just as certainly, are not as broad as those of Northern Cardinals.

Eastern Bluebirds are typically found in open habitats with scattered trees and shrubs. Such habitats provide good foraging for bluebirds, which usually capture their insect prey on the ground. The trees and shrubs provide hunting perches and cavities that can be used for nesting during the breeding season and for roosting during the nonbreeding season. Bluebirds can be less discriminating during the nonbreeding season, when the presence of a cavity is not essential. They are sometimes found in more wooded habitats during the nonbreeding season, because such areas may provide more fruit and berries and also provide greater protection from the elements.

A Michigan study revealed that Eastern Bluebirds were found in a variety of habitats during the winter, including pastures, open pine-oak woodlands, old fields, and residential areas, as well as farmland, cattle ranches, golf courses, orchards, clear-cut areas in forests, and reclaimed surface mines. These apparently diverse habitats share one characteristic of great importance to foraging bluebirds: low or sparse ground cover. The presence of scattered trees and shrubs for nest and roost sites might allow bluebirds to use such areas throughout the year.

3

Food and Feeding Habits

Birds have high metabolic rates, use energy at high rates, and as a result, must be efficient at locating and obtaining food. For bluebirds, that means consuming about 3 to 4 grams of food—or 10 to 12 percent of their body weight—each day. To put that in perspective, a 150-pound human with the metabolic rate of a bluebird would have to eat 15 to 18 pounds of food daily.

For bluebirds, the most important food is insects. Over an entire year, two-thirds or more of the food items eaten by bluebirds are insects. Among the most frequently eaten insects are beetles, grasshoppers and crickets, caterpillars, spiders, ants, and hemipterans (true bugs). Less often, bluebirds eat earthworms, millipedes, snails, and rarely, small snakes, lizards, and shrews.

Bluebirds prefer prey items of moderate size, $1/2$ to $1^1/4$ inches long; moderate consistency, not too hard or too soft; and with a smooth outer surface. Potential food items that are too large, too hard, too soft, or too bristly tend to be rejected by foraging bluebirds. Insects that taste bad, like ladybugs, or have formidable defenses, like adult praying mantises, may also be ignored. Very small insects such as leafhoppers are generally not taken because the cost is greater than the benefit—more energy is needed to capture them than is gained by eating them.

When insects are not available, such as during cold weather, bluebirds feed on a variety of fruits from trees, shrubs, vines, and herbaceous plants. These include flowering dogwood, American holly, hackberries, cherries, blackgum, red cedar, red mulberry, blackhaw, honey-

suckle, blackberry, raspberry, elderberry, sumac, blueberry, chokeberry, bittersweet, greenbriar, Virginia creeper, and common pokeberry. Some fruits provide more energy than others. For example, the fruit of a flowering dogwood represents about eight times more energy than a sumac fruit. Because bluebirds may spend 75 percent or more of their time foraging during periods of cold weather, the abundance and quality of fruits are of great importance to bluebirds wintering in the northern part of their range.

The diet of bluebirds varies with location and time of year. In the warmer parts of their range, Eastern Bluebirds depend more on insects throughout the year and less on fruits. Farther north, cold temperatures may limit the availability of insects, so bluebirds must eat more fruit during the winter months. The time of year with the coldest temperatures, December and January, is the time when bluebirds are most dependent on fruit.

Eastern Bluebirds use a variety of techniques to capture insects, depending on the type being hunted, the temperature, light conditions, and the availability of perches. Most often, bluebirds are classic sit-and-wait predators. Like many hawks and owls, bluebirds select an elevated perch that provides an unobstructed view and scan the ground for prey. When an insect is spotted, bluebirds drop to the ground and capture it with their bill. Also called drop hunting, this sit-and-wait technique is used most often by bluebirds in areas where perches are common and ground cover is sparse. Typical perches include utility lines and poles, fences and fence posts, dead or defoliated tree branches, small shrubs, and coarse weed stalks. Bluebirds may also use other perches, such as rooftops, road signs, garbage cans, or nesting boxes.

Successful drop hunting requires low, sparse vegetation, because bluebirds need a clear view of the ground. As vegetation grows taller and thicker, less ground is visible to a perched bluebird. Even if a bluebird spots an insect on the ground, taller, thicker vegetation can make it difficult for the bluebird to maneuver its way to the ground, and the cover provided by the vegetation may enable the targeted insect to avoid capture.

Perches may be as low as 2 feet or as high as 25 feet above the ground. When drop hunting in areas with low, sparse vegetation, bluebirds usually perch about 6 feet off the ground. As the temperature or light level decreases, so does perch height. During cooler weather and on overcast days, hunting bluebirds usually use lower perches. This is likely related to variation in the activity levels and visibility of potential insect prey. As temperatures decline, insects become less active and more difficult to locate. The diminished light of an overcast day also makes insects more difficult to spot. Perching closer to the ground in these cases improves a bluebird's chances of locating and capturing prey. Light levels may also influence insect activity levels. Direct sunlight may increase the temperature, particularly on the ground, and as a result, insect activity may increase. Active insects are more readily spotted, and bluebirds may use higher perches to increase their field of view.

Although drop-hunting bluebirds sometimes drop almost vertically to the ground, more often they take off at a slight angle and land several feet out from the point immediately below the perch. As this distance from the vertical increases, so does the distance between the bluebird and its potential prey item. Because insects are less active and more difficult to spot when temperatures are low, bluebirds not only use lower perches but tend to drop closer to their perches during the winter and early spring. As temperatures increase and insects become more active and easier to spot at greater distances, bluebirds tend to drop farther from their perches.

The distance that perched bluebirds drop, fly, or glide to prey items on the ground varies with temperature and, therefore, time of year. During colder weather, bluebirds typically attack insects 6 to 20 feet away. With warmer conditions, attack distances increase and typically range from 8 to 45 feet. When viewing conditions and insect activity are optimal, bluebirds can spot insects well over 100 feet away, possibly even as far as 200 feet.

Although bluebirds sometimes return to the same perch after an attack, more often they move to a different perch. The distance between successive perches varies with hunting success. In general, bluebirds tend to move farther when the previously used perch was unsuccessful.

Bluebirds typically spend 30 to 90 seconds on a perch before making an attack or moving to another perch. The length of time, however, varies with weather conditions. As temperatures decline, bluebirds tend to spend less time on each perch. In general, the need to obtain prey increases with decreasing temperatures, because the bird requires more energy to maintain body temperature. As a result, a bluebird may give up faster on a particular perch in an attempt to locate better foraging sites and maximize capture rates.

Once on the ground, bluebirds take the prey in their bill and either swallow it or carry it to a perch, depending on its size. Smaller prey, less than about $1/2$ inch long, is typically consumed on the ground; prey larger than that is usually taken to a perch. At the perch, bluebirds subdue and prepare a prey item for ingestion either by hammering it against the perch or by holding it in the bill and applying pressure using the cutting edges, or tomia, of the bill. While a bluebird is doing this, the prey sometimes escapes or is dropped. If this occurs, bluebirds drop from their perch, often with fluttering wings, and attempt to recapture the item. These recapture attempts are usually successful, and bluebirds sometimes recover the prey even before it reaches the ground.

Bluebirds are not always able to locate prey from their perches, particularly during colder weather, when insects are less abundant and less active. Perch success—the percentage of perches from which prey is spotted and a drop attack is initiated—can range from nearly 100 percent during the summer to less than 50 percent in late winter to early spring.

Another foraging tactic occasionally used by bluebirds is flycatching. A bluebird using this tactic flies from a perch in pursuit of a flying insect in the same manner as a tyrannid flycatcher, such as an Eastern Phoebe or Eastern Kingbird. These flycatching forays are usually short and almost always result in the capture of a single insect. Less often, perched bluebirds are opportunistic flycatchers and attempt to capture insects that just happen to fly by.

Bluebirds sometimes search for insects on the branches and leaves of trees and shrubs, a tactic referred to as gleaning. They most often glean when drop hunting. A perched bluebird scanning the ground for prey may spot an insect in a nearby shrub and, rather than making the typical drop to the ground, fly to and land in the shrub, where it gleans the insect from a branch or leaf. Insects that can be captured by gleaning include caterpillars, beetles, and ants. Infrequently, bluebirds flying to a shrub or tree may hover briefly and capture an insect without landing. This technique is appropriately called flight-gleaning.

Rarely, bluebirds forage by hopping along the ground in search of prey items. This hunting tactic may be used in areas with few suitable perches, such as recently plowed fields or large lawns, or, more likely, after landing on the ground while drop hunting. Unlike other thrushes, such as the American Robin, a bluebird searching for prey by hopping avoids areas with a lot of leaf litter and rarely, if ever, moves vegetation or litter with its bill or feet to expose prey items.

The foraging technique used least by Eastern Bluebirds is hovering because it's likely that more energy would be used while hovering than could be gained from any prey thus captured. Western Bluebirds and, especially, Mountain Bluebirds hover-forage more often than Eastern Bluebirds.

Bluebirds searching for insects and fruit rely on their keen vision. Enhancing this search is the ability of bluebirds to see near-ultraviolet (UV) light. Whereas human vision is limited to the visible spectrum of violet through red, many birds can detect shorter, or near-UV, wavelengths. This ability may be of great importance to foraging bluebirds, because some insects and berries may reflect near-UV light.

Bluebirds capture insects with their bills. The size and shape of bird bills differ among species and permit efficient use of particular food items. The Eastern Bluebird has a short, stout bill that, as is typical of thrushes, is slightly notched at the tip. Not designed for crushing seeds, the bluebird bill and associated jaw muscles permit efficient handling of fruit and, especially, insects. Although insects and fruits are swallowed whole, some preparation may be done prior to swallowing. The bird may remove the legs and wings of some insects and crush the head and thorax.

After a bluebird swallows, food items pass through the esophagus and into the stomach. A bird's stomach has two parts: an anterior portion, or proventriculus, which has a lining that secretes digestive juices, and a posterior portion, or gizzard, which has muscular walls and a hard, rough lining. Once food enters the gizzard, the muscular walls contract and relax, grinding and digesting hard food items.

After being pulverized in the gizzard, food passes into the intestine. Bluebirds and other primarily insectivorous birds have shorter intestines than seed-eating birds. Protein-rich foods like insects are partially digested by enzymes in the anterior portion of the stomach, so less time is needed to complete digestion in the intestine. In contrast, the stomach produces no enzymes that break down the fat and carbohydrate content of seeds and other plant material, and these foods must remain in the intestine for a

longer time to complete digestion. Once digested, food is absorbed through the walls of the intestine and distributed by the blood to the rest of the body.

Bluebirds can't digest some portions of the foods they consume, such as the exoskeletons of insects or the skins and seeds of fruits. As a result, they extract only a portion of the energy in the foods they eat. This low efficiency, coupled with the fact that the bluebird digestive system processes fruit very rapidly, means that bluebirds, particularly during cold weather, must eat large numbers of fruits.

Undigested materials are excreted in the feces. Among these materials are fruit seeds, which are generally viable. Bluebirds thus serve an important role as dispersers of many fruit-bearing plants.

Vocalizations

4

Many members of the thrush family, including the Wood Thrush, Hermit Thrush, and even the American Robin, produce beautiful and complex songs. Although not as well known as other thrushes for their vocalizations, the songs and singing behavior of Eastern Bluebirds are surprisingly complicated.

Bluebirds and other songbirds generally produce two types of vocalizations: songs and calls. Songs are relatively long in duration compared to most calls, are usually pleasing to the human ear, and typically play some role in reproduction. In contrast, calls are relatively short, acoustically simple vocalizations that serve a variety of functions.

The Eastern Bluebird uses its syrinx to produce a variety of calls, with different calls and their variants serving different functions. Among the best known and most frequently uttered call of bluebirds is the *tu-a-wee* call. This call is usually about 0.4 second in duration and, like most bluebird vocalizations, low in frequency. Both males and females, beginning as early as twelve days after hatching, give this call to inform other bluebirds of their location. Because the *tu-a-wee* calls of males are usually longer than those of females, a bluebird giving this call may also be providing information about its sex.

The *tu-a-wee* call is given in a variety of contexts, but most often when a bluebird's location is either changing or difficult to determine. A bluebird in flight often gives *tu-a-wee* calls, making it possible for other bluebirds to monitor the calling bird's location. Pairs, family groups, or flocks of bluebirds in areas with reduced visibility, such as along the edge of a woodlot, also use *tu-a-wee* calls to maintain contact.

Fledglings giving this call may be simultaneously advertising their hunger level and location to parents. Parents sometimes utter this call when coming to a nest box or cavity with food. Nestlings respond by extending their heads toward the cavity entrance and gaping. As a result, nestlings can be fed quickly, and the adult can spend more time foraging and less time at the nest, perhaps also reducing the likelihood of alerting predators to the presence of the nest.

Another call in the repertoire of bluebirds is the *chit,* or *chip,* call, which may be given singly or in a rapid series referred to as a chatter call. *Chit* calls may serve as alarm calls, with the level of alarm correlated with the rate of delivery. A single chit conveys mild alarm, while long chatters signal increasing alarm. Bluebirds utter *chit*s or chatters in several different contexts. During the breeding season, a bluebird chatters if a potential predator comes near a nest site. Here the chatters are likely directed at both family members and the intruder. In response, the mate can leave the nest box or cavity to avoid being trapped by the predator and help defend the nest site, and nestlings can reduce their chances of being discovered by crouching low and being quiet. The chattering may also divert the potential predator's attention to the calling bird and away from the nest site. At the same time, the calling bluebird may be warning the intruder about the probability of attack. If the intruder continues to move closer to a nest site, adult bluebirds may combine chatters with swoops or dives. As the predator continues its approach, the adults may give longer chatters at a faster rate while diving ever closer. In addition, the bluebirds may begin bill-snapping, rapidly closing their bills with sufficient force to create a sound, particularly as they approach the intruder during a dive. This change in vocal behavior, which no doubt is discerned by the predator, signals an increased likelihood of attack. Some predators, particularly smaller ones, may respond to this increased threat by retreating. Larger predators may not be deterred by the limited threat posed by such small birds and continue to the nest.

*Chit*s or chatters may also signal aggression when given in the presence of other bluebirds. Males may chatter during territorial disputes, and both males and females may chatter when other bluebirds, particularly those of the same sex, cross territorial boundaries and approach their nest site. Because suitable nest sites are essential for successful reproduction and may be in short supply, bluebirds can be surprisingly aggressive in defense of such sites. Here again, chatters may be given in combination with other aggressive behaviors, including dives, bill snaps, or even direct attacks, and the rate of calling and duration of chatters may increase with the level of aggression.

Another vocalization uttered by male and female bluebirds is the whine, or *turr,* call. This call, given more often by males, appears to signal the increased likelihood of an aggressive response. Male bluebirds engaged in territorial disputes with other males sometimes utter *turr* calls. *Turr* calls may serve as a warning to a nearby mate or fledglings when an aerial predator is nearby. *Turr* calls may also be uttered during the early stages of pair formation and in this context may signal appeasement.

Female bluebirds sometimes utter a low-volume *chip,* or *peep,* call when approached by a male during courtship and sometimes just prior to copulation. This call may serve as an appeasement signal, informing a male that he can safely approach the calling female.

Eastern Bluebirds also shriek, or scream, when held by a human or when captured and held by any other predator. Shrieks may be given singly or, more often, in a series. These are very high-volume calls with acoustic features that make the bird easy to locate. Many other kinds of birds also shriek when captured by predators. It is believed that these screams are meant to attract other, perhaps larger, predators that, in their attempts to take the shrieking bird from the original predator, may permit the bird to escape. Many studies have revealed that predators, including bluebird predators like Sharp-shinned Hawks and Cooper's Hawks, are attracted to distress screams. Although the likelihood that a screaming bluebird will escape from a predator is low, screaming may still be a better strategy than not screaming.

Juveniles utter screams when handled, captured, or nearly captured by potential predators. Adults are attracted to these screams and will vigorously attack a predator that has captured or is threatening to capture one of their young.

Young bluebirds also utter begging calls. These calls help adults monitor the hunger levels of their young and, after fledging, allow adults to locate their young. For about the first five days after hatching, young bluebirds utter high-frequency, low-volume *peep* calls, while extending their heads upward with open mouths. Because their eyes are closed, young nestlings *peep* in response to movement, such as when an adult arrives at the nest. After an adult leaves the nest or the adult female begins brooding, the nestlings again become quiet.

About five days after hatching, young bluebirds begin to develop a harsher-sounding *zeee* call. For a few days thereafter, nestlings may use both *peep* and *zeee* calls. With increasing age, the *zeee* call begins to predominate. Because their eyes are opening at about the same age, nestlings may utter *zeee* calls in response to a darkening of the nest box or cavity, as occurs when an adult arrives and blocks the entrance, as well as in response to movement. As with *peep* calls, *zeee* calls are just part of the begging response. While calling, nestlings also extend their open mouths toward the cavity entrance in an attempt to obtain food from a visiting adult. *Zeee* calls remain a part of a young bluebird's vocal repertoire until about four or five weeks posthatching. Young bluebirds typically leave the nest, or fledge, sixteen to twenty-two days after hatching, so *zeee* calls can still be heard a week or two after fledging.

Prior to fledging, when about twelve to fourteen days old, young bluebirds also begin to utter *tu-a-wee* calls. Shortly after fledging, therefore, both *zeee* and *tu-a-wee* calls provide adults with information about the hunger levels and location of their young.

Arthur Cleveland Bent observed that the bluebird "cannot compete with the greater songsters of the famous thrush family; but his short contralto notes . . . are most welcome and pleasing to the ear, full of richness and sweetness." A single bluebird song often sounds something like *turwy, cherwee, cherey-lew.* In contrast to most other songbirds, female bluebirds sing as well, although not as often, as males.

The songs of Eastern Bluebirds are relatively low in frequency and volume, and short in duration, ranging from 0.5 to 2 seconds. Each song is made up of subunits called notes, most songs consisting of two, three, or four notes. Rarely do songs include more than ten notes. Although most notes are brief, modulated whistles, there is considerable variation among different notes in frequency, duration, and number of modulations. Each bluebird possesses a very large repertoire, perhaps hundreds of different note types, and particular note types are rarely repeated within a song. Because bluebirds have large note repertoires and use different combinations of notes in different songs, they can produce many different songs, called song types. Male bluebirds in central Kentucky were found to use an average of sixty different song types over an entire breeding season. Even that number, large compared to the number of different song types used by most male songbirds, is deceptively low, because new song types were used almost every time the bluebirds were observed. Additional observation time would certainly have revealed additional song types. It appears, therefore, that male bluebirds have very large song type repertoires, possibly numbering in the hundreds. In fact, the song type repertoires of male bluebirds may not even be fixed. They may, in the same manner as a few other birds such as Northern Mockingbirds, continue to create new note types and song types.

The large song repertoires of male Eastern Bluebirds, and males of other species as well, may be the result of female preferences. In some species, such as Red-winged Blackbirds, Northern Mockingbirds, and European Starlings, the size of a male's song repertoire is correlated with age. Older males may have larger repertoires if time is required to learn or develop new song types. From a female's perspective, repertoire size may be important because older males are likely to outcompete younger males for resources such as good-quality territories. If so, then repertoire size would be an indicator of male quality. Although this is an attractive hypothesis, the possible relationships among male age, repertoire size, quality, and female preferences in Eastern Bluebirds are unknown.

Male Eastern Bluebirds may sing occasionally in February, but sustained singing begins in March and continues into August. As days become longer in February and March, an area of the brain called the hypothalamus releases hormones that in turn stimulate the pituitary gland. Pituitary hormones then cause the testes to increase in size and release the hormone testosterone. Testosterone stimulates growth of the areas in the brain that control singing behavior, and male bluebirds begin to sing. Initially, males may not sing much because testosterone levels are still low and weather conditions may inhibit singing. When temperatures are low, male bluebirds must spend more time foraging and have less time and energy for singing. As days lengthen and temperatures rise, the combined effects of more testosterone and increased availability of food generate higher singing rates.

Beyond physiology and food, the singing rates of male bluebirds also vary with mated status and breeding stage. Unpaired males sing most persistently and at the highest rates, averaging about four hundred to five hundred songs per hour. For brief periods, males may utter one thousand or more songs per hour. Males seeking mates don't sing continuously, but alternate periods of singing—often fifteen to fifty minutes in duration—with feeding and other activities.

Male bluebirds continue to sing after pairing, but rates decline to perhaps one hundred to two hundred songs per hour. Later in the nesting cycle, when mates are incubating or both members of a pair are feeding nestlings or fledglings, males sing even less, averaging fifty to one hundred songs per hour. Late in the breeding season, male singing rates may remain low even after young become independent. However, if a nest with eggs or young is lost to predation early in the breeding season, females begin a new nest within a few days, and during the interval between nests, male singing rates increase dramatically. Rates during this time are comparable to rates immediately after pairing and prior to initiation of a pair's first nest, averaging one hundred to three hundred songs per hour.

When singing, male bluebirds often use high, exposed perches, because such locations make it easier to observe potential predators and nearby bluebirds and maximize sound transmission. Typical perches include the tops of dead trees and utility lines and poles. An unpaired male may leave his singing perch when a potential mate enters the territory and, while continuing to sing, fly toward the female or a potential nest site. Singing may then continue from a perch near the female or from a nest cavity or box.

While it has long been recognized that many birds sing to attract mates and establish territories, recent studies have revealed that singing can also serve other functions. Males in some species may sing to solicit extrapair copulations, deter other males from copulating with their mates, coordinate activities around the nest, stimulate the reproductive activity of mates, and help maintain contact with mates or offspring. The singing of male bluebirds probably serves many of these functions.

Before pairing in the spring, or after losing a mate during the breeding season, male bluebirds sing at higher rates and volumes. Unpaired males also use a variety of different song types when singing. After pairing, male bluebirds sing fewer, lower-volume songs and use fewer song types. These changes clearly indicate that one function of singing by male bluebirds is mate attraction.

Just as clearly, singing by male bluebirds plays a role in territorial defense. In early spring, males sometimes engage in song duels with neighboring males when territory boundaries are being established. During such duels, males perch near the contested boundary and sing with higher-than-usual volume. Male bluebirds also sing in response to territorial intrusions by other males. Even simulated intrusions, whereby a recording of bluebird songs is played in a male's territory, will elicit singing by male bluebirds intent on defending their territory. Such responses indicate that singing by male bluebirds is sometimes directed at other males and sends a "stay out of my territory" message.

After establishing territories and attracting mates, male bluebirds continue to sing, although at lower rates and volumes, suggesting that singing serves additional functions. Because low volume reduces transmission distance, much of the singing by male bluebirds after pairing is probably not meant to be heard by bluebirds beyond the territory boundaries but is directed at mates. Shortly after pairing, females are likely engaged in prenesting activities, such as nest building. Singing by males during this time may serve to stimulate females. Male singing rates among bluebirds and other species tend to increase later in the breeding season, when the female initiates a new nest after losing a nest to a predator or after young from the previous nest have fledged. This resurgence of song may be important in stimulating the hormonal changes in females that eventually lead to ovulation and egg laying.

Both male and female bluebirds may sing when a potential predator approaches a nest. These songs, generally high in volume and preceded by one or more *chit* or click notes, serve to inform a mate and any nestlings that a predator is nearby. When so alerted, the mate may approach to help defend the nest.

The acquisition of song by Eastern Bluebirds and other songbirds begins at an early age. During their first summer and fall, young bluebirds listen to the songs of adults and may memorize some of the notes and songs for future use. Occasionally, young bluebirds may even produce low-volume sounds that, although bearing limited resemblance to adult songs, are the forerunners of song. Following the summer and fall learning and listening period, young bluebirds then enter a silent period, extending from late fall through early winter, during which they don't attempt to sing.

Beginning in January or February, young Eastern Bluebirds, particularly males, may once again begin to sing, although the singing during this period is low in volume and rambling, with little resemblance to typical adult song. This unstructured singing, called subsong, is not meant to communicate any information, but represents practice. Although young bluebirds may attempt to reproduce notes or songs uttered by nearby adults, plus those heard the previous summer and fall, there also appears to be much improvisation. Young bluebirds may modify previously heard notes and create new ones. Subsong may continue for several weeks; during this time, singing gradually becomes more adultlike. By now, young bluebirds have a unique repertoire of notes and song types.

Because song development by young bluebirds involves improvisation and, apparently, the creation of new notes and song types, individuals in a particular area share few song types. Because each male bluebird, and probably female as well, has a unique repertoire, its mate and neighboring bluebirds are likely able to recognize the songs and identify the singing individual. One advantage to this is that time and energy are not wasted by unnecessary responses to singing bluebirds that represent little or no threat. A new bluebird moving into an area sings different, unrecognized songs, and resident birds respond aggressively, as a new bluebird moving into or passing through an area may seek to usurp a territory or mate and does represent a threat.

Behavior

LOCOMOTION

Eastern Bluebirds spend most of their time in open areas. Their wings are not as long and narrow as those of fast fliers, such as swallows or swifts, but not as short and wide as those of birds that fly through dense underbrush, such as grouse or quail. As a result, bluebirds are very maneuverable yet can fly at reasonably high speeds—up to 45 miles per hour if necessary.

Eastern Bluebirds spend most of their time on perches but do come to the ground to forage, drink, or bathe. They have typical songbird feet, with three toes projecting forward, and one backward. The toes have curved nails that help the birds grip small branches. When moving about on the ground, bluebirds hop rather than walk.

SELF-MAINTENANCE

Feathers serve many functions. They create the streamlining needed for flight, and wing feathers provide both lift and propulsion. Feathers also protect a bird's skin and play an important role in thermoregulation. To ensure that their feathers continue to serve these functions, bluebirds keep them in good shape by preening. They clean the larger feathers, such as the tail and flight feathers, by drawing them through the bill. While preening, bluebirds also use the bill to apply secretions from the uropygial, or preen, gland. These oily secretions contain a mixture of waxes, fatty acids, fat, and water and help preserve feather moistness and flexibility. They also help protect feathers from bacteria and fungi. Preening bluebirds also remove feather parasites.

Bathing also helps bluebirds keep their feathers in good condition, removing dust and dirt as well as feather parasites. When bathing, a bluebird typically lowers its head and breast into the water and shakes its bill from side to side, sometimes beating both wings. Then it raises its head and breast while lowering its rump into the water and simultaneously spreads its tail and flutters its wings. How often bluebirds bathe in the wild is unknown, but those in captivity bathe every day.

Bluebirds also sunbathe. When sunbathing, they ruffle their plumage and may spread their tail feathers and extend one or both wings. On cold days, sunbathing provides heat from solar radiation. Bluebirds also sunbathe on very warm days; the heat may cause increased movement by feather parasites, making it easier for a preening bluebird to remove them.

ROOSTING AND SLEEPING

Eastern Bluebirds spend much of their time roosting, either resting or sleeping. Roost sites, especially those used when sleeping, are generally on branches of trees that provide good cover. For short periods of rest, roost sites may be in more open locations. During the nonbreeding season, typically during periods of cold weather, bluebirds may roost overnight in cavities or nest boxes.

Family or flock members often roost together, each bluebird usually remaining about 2 feet from other individuals, a distance referred to as individual distance. Rarely, bluebirds, particularly fledglings, will roost right next to each other on a tree branch during very cold weather.

When roosting, a bluebird often fluffs its feathers, with head drawn in and bill slightly elevated. It may also bend its legs so its body rests on the perch. One foot is sometimes lifted and tucked into the ventral feathers; this helps reduce heat loss from the feet and legs during cold weather.

Sites typically selected for nocturnal roosting and sleeping are similar to those selected for roosting during the day—high in trees on branches that provide good cover. At nocturnal roosts, bluebirds spend some time sleeping, but they're probably awake much of the time as well, especially during the warmer months. Spending as much time awake as possible may reduce the likelihood of being captured by a nocturnal predator.

NONVOCAL COMMUNICATION

Perches, territories, nest sites, and mates are important resources for bluebirds, and depending on the circumstances, bluebirds may attempt to gain access to these resources using aggression. However, because aggression costs more in terms of time, energy, and risk of injury, blue-birds use signals to reduce the likelihood that an aggressive interaction will escalate into actual fighting. These signals simply convey a threat of aggres-sion, ranging from those that communicate a limited threat to those that communicate a much greater threat.

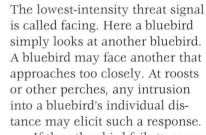

The lowest-intensity threat signal is called facing. Here a bluebird simply looks at another bluebird. A bluebird may face another that approaches too closely. At roosts or other perches, any intrusion into a bluebird's individual dis-tance may elicit such a response.

If the other bird fails to move away or continues to approach, a bluebird may escalate the encounter with a head-forward display. During this display, a bluebird sleeks its head and neck feathers and leans forward. If the encounter continues, the increasing threat of attack may be conveyed by gaping, bill-snapping, or even lunging at the other bluebird.

When gaping, a bluebird faces another and holds its bill open for several seconds. If an interaction escalates, the bird opens its bill even wider. This display, when combined with bill snaps and rasp calls, signals a high likelihood of attack. Low-intensity gaping is sometimes observed during the early stages of pair formation, as when a female gapes slightly when a male intent on courtship feeding approaches with food.

Another aggressive display that signals a high likelihood of attack is wing-flicking, in which bluebirds rapidly flick both wings away from and back to the body. While wing-flicking, bluebirds often utter chatter calls and tail fan, rapidly fanning the tail feathers in and out. This display may be used when other bluebirds trespass into a pair's territory. Territorial bluebirds closely approaching an intruder may first begin wing-flicking, along with chattering and tail-fanning; if the intruder maintains its position, they may then attack.

Initially, an attacking bluebird flies at and supplants, or takes over the perch of, the other individual. During the approach, the attacking bluebird may also bill-snap. If the supplanted bluebird remains nearby, several supplanting attacks may follow in rapid succession. If the bird takes flight as the aggressor approaches, a chase may ensue.

Supplanting attacks accompanied by chases often occur when a bluebird intrudes into another's territory. After being supplanted one or more times, a trespasser may be chased from the territory. If territorial ownership is in doubt, however, as may be the case early in the breeding season, the encounter may continue to escalate into fighting.

During a fight, bluebirds strike with their wings, peck at each other's heads, and attempt to grab each other with their feet. When so engaged, bluebirds often tumble about on the ground. Fights are usually brief and rarely lead to serious injuries.

Most bluebird fights are disputes with other bluebirds of the same sex over territories and nest sites. Bluebirds will also attack—and less often, fight—birds of other species, particularly other cavity nesters such as House Sparrows, European Starlings, Carolina Chickadees, Tree Swallows, and Great Crested Flycatchers.

Bluebirds may choose to avoid aggressive interactions and perform appeasement displays. One simple display is turning away, in which a bluebird fluffs its body feathers and turns its head or entire body away from another bird. This display may be used during the early stages of pair formation when a male and female first approach each other, as during a male's initial attempts at courtship feeding, or when two males or females perch near each other during an encounter at a territory boundary.

Another appeasement display is the fluffed posture display. This display is subtle; a perched bluebird assumes a normal posture but fluffs its plumage and points its bill slightly upward. The key element of this display is fluffing the plumage; this appears to convey submission and reduces the likelihood of attack.

Eastern Bluebirds also use a variety of visual displays during courtship. The oblique sleek display is usually given near the nest site. As a female and potential mate approaches the nest site, the male turns his back to her with plumage sleeked, wings drooping, bill slightly raised, and tail spread. By doing so, the male bluebird is providing information about his quality to the female. As courtship continues, the male may lift and quiver his wings during this display and may also sing.

In the wings-raised sleek display, a crouching male faces a female with plumage sleeked and wings raised to or above the shoulders. He spreads his tail, slightly raises his bill, in which he may be carrying nesting material, and may utter low-volume songs. This display usually lasts less than five seconds and is often performed near a nest site. During the early stages of pair formation, a male bluebird sometimes performs a wings-raised sleek display before a nest demonstration display. After pairing, a male may, for unknown reasons, attack his mate after a wings-raised sleek display.

Among the more obvious court-ship displays of male Eastern Bluebirds is wing-flicking, or wing-waving. During this display, a male lifts one or both wings up and away from the body. Depending on the intensity of the display, this flicking may occur at different speeds. At highest intensity, both wings are held out, fully extended, then moved up and down. A male wing-flicks when his mate or a prospective mate approaches. Before pairing, wing-flicking, often accompanied by singing, makes a male more conspicuous and perhaps more likely to attract the attention of a female.

After pairing, wing-flicking acts as a greeting between members of a pair.

Male bluebirds also use aerial displays to attract the attention of females. During courtship, males sometimes perform rapid flight song displays. While flying rapidly between perches, one of which is typically a cavity or nest box, males sing. This display is most often performed by unpaired males. A male that loses his mate at some point during the breeding season may begin performing rapid flight song displays in an attempt to obtain a new mate.

During pair formation, males may perform the butterfly flight, in which the wings are extended and the tail is spread. This display is often accompanied by song. Males beat their wings more slowly than usual, and as a result, they fly rather slowly. Butterfly flights usually end at a nest cavity or box and so advertise not only the presence of a male but a nest site as well.

Once a male bluebird has attracted the attention of a female, the nest demonstration display is performed to further advertise himself and a nest site. This display is an important part of pair formation and after pairing may help strengthen the pair-bond. When a female is nearby, a male flies to a nest cavity or box and perches at the entrance with tail spread and wings open, clearly displaying his blue back, wings, and tail. At the entrance, the male may look into the cavity or box and, with a rocking motion, alternately move his head and shoulders into and out of the entrance. The male may then enter the cavity or box and peer out from the entrance. Once he exits, the male may quickly turn in midair, hover briefly, land at the entrance again, and repeat the display. At other times, a male leaves the cavity or box, flies to the top of the nest box or to a perch above the cavity, or sometimes to a more distant perch, and begins to sing. This may be followed by a flight back to the cavity or box entrance, or to another one elsewhere in the territory, where he repeats the display. The intensity of nest demonstration displays varies. A male may simply fly to a cavity entrance, peer in, and then leave. Males often sing and carry nest material during the display.

Female bluebirds, both paired and unpaired, take an active part in the nest demonstration display. When performed by an unpaired male, the response of the female determines whether pairing occurs. A female that simply remains perched during the male's display or one that flies to the cavity or box entrance but fails to enter is not going to form a pair-bond. As a male displays, a female bluebird may make an initial approach to the cavity or box entrance, perch briefly, but then, rather than entering, fly to another perch within the male's territory and preen, or in some other way appear to ignore the male. As the male continues displaying, the female, sometimes uttering an occasional song, may begin moving closer to the cavity or box.

Eventually, when the male is inside the cavity or box, the female again flies to the entrance and looks in, but may or may not enter. If she doesn't enter, she again flies to another perch, and the process is repeated, perhaps several times. Finally, the female approaches, perches at the entrance, and enters the cavity or box while the male is inside. This act appears to be a critical step in pair formation. Once accomplished, the male and female are almost certain to pair. The male exits the cavity or box first and flies to a nearby perch, where he often performs an oblique sleek display. The female

follows and usually supplants the male. The pair then continues with the nest demonstration display, in which both participate, often at different potential nest sites in the male's territory.

Before or, more often, after pairing, male bluebirds may also engage in courtship feeding. This behavior has been observed in many species of songbirds, including Eastern Bluebirds, and as the name suggests, this behavior may occur during pair formation. However, male bluebirds feed their mates much more often during nest building, egg laying, and incubation. Sometimes the male simply flies to a female and attempts to feed her. At other times, a female bluebird resembles a begging fledgling as she utters begging calls and lifts one or both wings in rapid succession. This begging can be most effective. One investigator noted that many food items that males would otherwise eat themselves were given to females because of their persistent begging. Courtship feeding during pair formation or early in the nesting cycle may provide females with important information about a male, particularly his foraging skills. But because most courtship feeding actually occurs during the period just prior to egg laying, the more important function of this feeding is to help female bluebirds meet the energy demands of egg laying. Food provided by males not only gives a female an extra source of energy, but also reduces the time she must spend foraging. That saves a female additional energy and time, which she can spend near, and perhaps defending, the nest site.

Female bluebirds indicate their readiness to copulate with a solicit display. A low-intensity version of the solicit display may be performed by females during courtship; this version rarely leads to successful copulation. During the low-intensity solicit, the female crouches with her plumage compressed, head drawn in, bill slightly raised, wings drooping, and tail slightly raised. The male responds by flying to and landing on the female's back, often pecking at her head. After pairing, and as the time of egg laying approaches, the female performs a high-intensity solicit display that precedes successful copulation: crouching with plumage compressed, bill slightly raised, wings drooped and sometimes quivering, and tail held high. The male responds by flying to the female and landing either directly on her back or next to her and then getting on her back. He then waves his wings and brings his tail down to make cloacal contact. As is true for most birds, bluebird copulations are brief, lasting just one to five seconds. Females solicit and pairs copulate several times for each clutch of eggs. Not all copulations involve paired bluebirds: females sometimes copulate with other males, often neighboring ones. Most copulations occur during the week before the first egg of a clutch is laid.

SPACING

Eastern Bluebirds defend all-purpose territories—territories within which mating (at least within-pair mating), nesting, and feeding take place. Territories are defended only during the breeding season, generally beginning in February or March and extending through August or September. The size of bluebird territories varies with habitat quality, including number of nest sites, and population density. Territories average about 5 or 6 acres but can be as large as 20 acres.

With the breakup of winter flocks or arrival of migrants at the breeding grounds, male Eastern Bluebirds begin to sing, and interactions between males become more frequent. Territories are established by singing, displays, chases, and fights. Female bluebirds also help defend territories by patrolling boundaries and chasing and attacking intruding females. Intruders are often attacked, and such attacks are almost always by individuals of the same sex. In areas with high densities of males, territorial boundaries may be very well defined. With decreasing densities, boundaries may become less precise. Boundaries also fluctuate during the breeding season. The size of territories decreases as the nesting period progresses, with males spending more time near nest sites as they guard mates or feed young. Territories may also diminish as insect foods become increasingly available.

Bluebirds occasionally trespass into nearby territories to gain access to particular resources, such as food or water, to determine the nesting status of neighboring individuals, or to seek partners for extrapair copulations.

As the breeding season ends, the intensity of territorial defense declines, and trespassing by other bluebirds, especially fledglings, occurs more frequently. By September or October, territorial boundaries are no longer defended, although resident pairs may remain near their breeding territories during the nonbreeding season and may continue to defend nest sites, which they sometimes use as roost sites.

6

The Breeding Season

Throughout their range, the breeding season of Eastern Bluebirds extends from February through August, although there are regional differences in timing, with bluebirds farther south initiating breeding activities before those to the north. Male bluebirds sing to establish territories and attract mates during February and March, and nest building begins sometime between early March and mid-April. The nesting season usually ends by late July but may extend into September for bluebirds in the northern part of their range.

For bluebirds, as for many other birds that breed in temperate areas, it's important to start nesting as soon as possible. Earlier breeders are usually more successful, producing more young that are more likely to survive. Bluebirds that get an early start with their first nest are more likely to have time for a second nesting attempt and may be able to produce more young during the breeding season. Young from earlier broods have more time to develop their skills, including foraging skills. These older, often larger juveniles tend to dominate smaller, less experienced young from later nests and thus are more likely to survive.

Nest predators may be less active or even absent early in the breeding season. House Wrens migrate to their breeding areas several weeks after bluebirds, and early-nesting bluebirds may be able to successfully raise a brood of young before the wrens even arrive. Insects that occasionally contribute to bluebird nest failure, such as ants and blowflies, may also be less of a problem early in the breeding season.

Given these advantages of early breeding, why don't all bluebirds do so? One important factor is age. Older bluebirds usually begin breeding before younger bluebirds, especially first-time breeders. Young males are often at a competitive disadvantage when attempting to establish territories. In the southern part of their range, older male bluebirds can remain in or near their territories from previous years and can quickly reestablish dominance in these territories as the breeding season begins. Young males may have to look for

open territories and as a result may establish territories later than the older males. Similarly, older bluebirds may pair up before first-year birds, pairing with their mates from the previous year, and re-forming a pair-bond takes less time than forming a new one.

Older birds are typically better foragers than first-year birds, because they have more experience. As a result, older birds are usually in better physical condition and have larger energy reserves than younger birds. This may mean that older birds can migrate to breeding areas before younger birds. In addition, reproduction requires substantial amounts of energy; once on the breeding grounds, young bluebirds may require more time to acquire the necessary energy.

Throughout much of their range, pairs of bluebirds attempt to raise at least two broods during the breeding season. However, those breeding in northern areas, such as Canada and New England, may have time to raise only a single brood, whereas those farther south are sometimes able to raise three broods.

Most bluebird nests fledge at least one young, but success varies among locations and years and is influenced by several factors, including predator density, numbers of nest-site competitors, and weather. Studies have revealed no consistent geographic trends in bluebird nesting success.

Overall, it is likely that at least 60 percent of all bluebird nests are successful. This is typical for secondary cavity nesters—birds that nest in cavities but do not actually create the cavities. In contrast, many primary cavity nesters—species that nest in and make their own cavities, such as woodpeckers—have success rates of 70 to 85 percent. The lower success rate of secondary cavity nesters may be due to predators that remember the locations of previously used cavities or boxes from one year to the next.

The most common predators of bluebird eggs and nestlings in many areas are raccoons and black rat snakes. Raccoons typically climb to a cavity or box at night, reaching in through the entrance and pulling out incubating or brooding females, eggs, or nestlings. Rat snakes may be active at any time of the day or night. They are excellent climbers and can reach almost any cavity or box. Once inside, the snakes eat incubating or brooding females, eggs, or nestlings. Because raccoons and rat snakes forage along habitat edges, a series of bluebird boxes along a fence row may be particularly susceptible to these predators.

Other nest predators include cats, eastern chipmunks, flying squirrels, red squirrels, bull snakes, black racers, milk snakes, eastern coachwhips, and garter snakes. Cats are incredibly effective predators; in the United States, they kill several hundred million birds every year.

Much smaller organisms are sometimes responsible for nest failure. Ants sometimes discover bluebird cavities or boxes. In the southern United States, foraging fire ants that locate a bluebird nest will kill and eat any nestlings present. Other, less aggressive species of ants may move into bluebird cavities or boxes. If this occurs during nest building or incubation, the bluebirds are likely to abandon the nest. If ants move in when bluebirds are caring for nestlings, ant activity will likely be concentrated in and below the nest, and the young bluebirds, although suffering occasional bites or stings, may survive to fledging.

Bluebird nest failure sometimes results from the activities of other species of birds. Three species are competitors for nest sites: House Wrens (pictured here), House Sparrows, and European Starlings. Wrens sometimes puncture bluebird eggs or, less often, kill bluebird nestlings. Eggs so destroyed by wrens typically have a single small hole left by the wren's bill. Wrens sometimes remove the damaged eggs or dead nestlings from the nest cavity or box. Wrens do not actually eat the eggs or nestlings; the purpose of their depredations is to increase the number of potential wren nest sites.

House Sparrows are well-known nest-site competitors of Eastern Bluebirds. Bluebirds recognize the threat posed by House Sparrows, and both males and females may respond aggressively to the presence of a sparrow near a nest site. Bluebirds have attacked models of House Sparrows experimentally placed near nest sites. These attacks can be intense, with bluebirds sometimes perching on the models and vigorously pecking at the head. Such aggression is potentially advantageous, because House Sparrows may destroy bluebird eggs, kill nestlings, or even kill adult bluebirds occupying a nest cavity or box. House Sparrows kill nestling and adult bluebirds by repeatedly pecking at the head and inflicting lethal head wounds. Again, the purpose of such behavior is to increase the number of available nest sites.

European Starlings are yet another nest-site competitor, and they will almost always destroy bluebird eggs and kill nestlings in an attempt to limit competition for available nest cavities or boxes. However, because they weigh more than twice as much as bluebirds, starlings are not always able to fit through the entrances of bluebird cavities or boxes. If bluebirds are nesting in such sites, starlings represent less of a threat than House Sparrows or House Wrens.

Inclement weather is responsible for the failure of some bluebird nests, particularly early nests in the northern part of their range. Periods of cold, wet weather can lead to nest failure; embryos or nestlings may die of exposure if their body temperatures get too low. Normally, adult females prevent this by incubating eggs or brooding nestlings. Cold, wet weather can reduce prey availability, however, compelling adults to spend more time foraging and less time on the nest. This results in less parental attention and, in the case of nestlings, less food, and may eventually cause the death of embryos or nestlings.

The response of bluebirds after losing a nest varies with sex and time of year. Female bluebirds often abandon a territory and mate after such a loss. Females that lose the first nest of the breeding season are particularly likely to abandon. Less likely to desert are females that have had one successful nest and lose the second. Such females may remain and attempt a third nest at a different site. Male bluebirds, especially those that have nested in the territory previously, are less likely to leave after a nest failure. Unless it's very late in the breeding season, a male left behind after being abandoned by a female will begin singing at an increased rate to attract a new mate.

There are good reasons for a female bluebird to abandon a territory after losing a nest. The nest loss may reflect the quality of a male and his territory. A better-quality male may have been able to successfully defend the nest. If so, the female may be better off with a different mate. Also, the presence of a predator, especially one that may now associate cavities or nest boxes with something to eat, represents more of a threat to a female bluebird than to a male, because incubating or brooding females spend much more time in nest cavities or boxes. A female may be better off abandoning a territory with a known predator and seeking a new territory elsewhere.

Eastern Bluebirds, like most other bird species, are considered monogamous, as most individuals form a pair-bond with just one member of the opposite sex. Less than 3 percent of male bluebirds are polygynous, pairing with two females. The pair-bonds of bluebirds sometimes last for an entire breeding season, although they may be shorter in duration, sometimes lasting for just one breeding attempt, or longer, extending over two or more breeding seasons.

Bluebird pair-bonds are usually formed during February and early March. Occasionally, pairs form or re-form prior to the breakup of winter flocks. More typically, pair formation occurs after males establish territories. Males that arrive on breeding territories unpaired are typically, though not always, paired within a week. Female bluebirds associate with territorial males to examine the quality of the male and his territory. If a male or his territory is of insufficient quality, the female simply moves to another territory.

To attract the attention of females, male bluebirds seeking mates sing at high rates. An unpaired male spotting a female in his territory sings at higher rates and begins displaying to draw her attention to his plumage—and perhaps quality—as well as potential nest sites. An interested female eventually follows the male to a nest cavity or box. After the male enters, she may then fly to the entrance. If, based on her examination of the male and his territory, she decides to pair with him, she joins him inside. Once this occurs, the two bluebirds are paired.

7

Nest Building, Egg Laying, and Incubation

Although they use cavities for nesting, Eastern Bluebirds are unable to create or excavate their own. They are dependent on the work of primary cavity nesters—birds that actually excavate cavities. The most prevalent primary cavity nesters are woodpeckers, which come in various sizes and therefore excavate cavities of various sizes. Woodpeckers that produce cavities potentially suitable for bluebirds include Northern Flickers and Red-bellied, Downy, and Hairy Woodpeckers.

In a Virginia study, forty-three of forty-seven bluebird nests found in natural cavities were in ones excavated by Downy or Hairy Woodpeckers or Northern Flickers. A Michigan study found that seventy-six of ninety-eight natural-cavity bluebird nest sites (78 percent) were located in abandoned woodpecker cavities and that bluebirds preferred the abandoned cavities of smaller woodpeckers, such as downies. This use of smaller entrances and cavities may represent a true preference, perhaps because smaller entrances would exclude more potential predators, or may have been the result of competition by larger cavity nesters, such as European Starlings.

Bluebirds use natural cavities in many different trees, living or dead, including oaks, elms, apple, black cherry, locusts, ashes, and willows. In addition to woodpecker cavities, bluebirds may use cavities created by natural decay or fire. Much less frequently, bluebirds may nest in crevices or holes near the bases of cliffs or in vertical rock walls created by road building or mining.

The characteristics of natural sites used by bluebirds may vary greatly. Cavity entrances may be anywhere from 2 to nearly 60 feet above ground, with most 4 to 20 feet high. The entrance openings of natural sites range from about 1.4 to 5 inches in diameter, with 1.5 to 3 inches most typical. The entrances to some natural cavities, especially those resulting from decay, may not be circular. The interiors of natural cavities vary in volume; those used by bluebirds usually have inner diameters of 3 to 4 inches and are 5 to 9 inches deep. When nesting in deeper cavities, bluebirds often add more material to get the top of the nest closer to the entrance. Commonly, the top of a bluebird nest, even in a deep cavity, is only about 3 to 6 inches from the entrance.

In some areas, particularly in the northern part of their range, the entrances of natural cavities used by bluebirds are often oriented to the southeast. This may be beneficial because a southeast exposure provides protection from prevailing winds and storms and exposes the front of the nest cavity to the early-morning sun, which may be particularly valuable during periods of cool weather early in the breeding season. Because bluebirds are secondary cavity nesters, the orientation of their natural nest sites is largely dependent on the preferences of the woodpeckers that originally excavated the cavities.

Natural cavities suitable for use by Eastern Bluebirds are in short supply, because landowners often cut down dead trees and remove dead branches from live trees. The use of metal fence posts has also eliminated another source of suitable cavities—decaying wooden fence posts, which at one time dotted the countryside. And the natural cavities that are available may be usurped by other secondary cavity nesters, such as House Sparrows, European Starlings, Tree Swallows, and House Wrens.

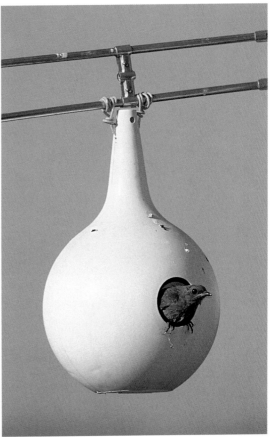

Fortunately, bluebirds also nest in a variety of man-made structures: nest boxes built specifically for their use, as well as mailboxes, drainpipes, empty jars and cans, hollow posts, even the barrel of a cannon at the University of Minnesota. Bluebirds will use a wide variety of nest containers, including those made of wood, half-gallon milk cartons, plastic gallon jugs, PVC pipe, and, rarely, gourds.

Because nest location can influence nesting success, female bluebirds likely select cavities or boxes with characteristics that provide the greatest chances of success: entrances just large enough to permit passage of bluebirds and a height that is out of reach of ground-based predators. Bluebirds are most likely to use nest cavities or boxes in large open areas with sparse or short ground cover, a few trees or shrubs for perching, and well away from woodland edges and water. Such sites provide good foraging habitat; reduced competition from House Wrens, typically found in areas with more woody vegetation, and Tree Swallows, which prefer sites near water; and less of a threat from predators found along woodland edges or in areas with more ground cover, such as many species of snakes.

After pair formation, the female bluebird, generally accompanied by the male, visits potential nest sites. Both male and female fly to the cavity entrances, sometimes carrying small amounts of nest material. These inspection visits often include wing-waving and singing by the male. Either member of the pair may enter cavities during these visits, and if so, any nest material carried in is typically left behind. While inside, a bluebird may simply look around the interior, perhaps pecking lightly at the walls of the cavity. The female bluebird sometimes makes nest-shaping movements, even when little or no nest material is present. This may provide a female with important information concerning the size, depth, and volume of the cavity.

Although both sexes inspect potential nest sites, the final decision is made by the female. This is appropriate because female bluebirds have more at stake. Females spend much more time in the nest cavity or box than their mate, and a low-quality nest site could both reduce the chances of successfully fledging young and increase the risk to a female from predators.

For the first nest of the year, actual nest building begins from several days to six weeks after a site is chosen. Later in the breeding season, this interval is shorter. Construction of a bluebird nest usually takes four to seven days but can take as long as twenty, depending on the time of year and the weather. The first nest of the season usually takes longer to build, often eight to twelve days. Later in the season, nest construction often takes just two to five days. This difference may be due in part to weather conditions. During cool, wet weather in early spring, females need to spend more time foraging and have less time for nest construction. In addition, some females begin construction of more than one nest. In most cases, these extra nests are not completed, but this additional effort slows down the construction of the nest that will actually be used. At any time of year, inclement weather slows down the rate of nest construction, and construction stops completely during heavy rain.

Only the female builds the nest. Males occasionally bring nest material to the cavity or box but rarely help with the actual construction. Females gathering nest material are often accompanied by their mates. This serves at least two functions. First, females may be more vulnerable to predation when preoccupied by nest construction, and their mates can alert them to the presence of potential predators. Second, females are fertile during nest construction, and a male nearby may be able to reduce the chances that his mate will engage in extrapair copulations.

   Most nest building, especially for the first nest of the season, occurs in the morning. Late in the breeding season, females may work on nest construction throughout much of the day. This work involves locating and carrying nest material to the nest site and fashioning it into a cup-shaped nest. The amount of material needed depends on the volume of the cavity or box.

Bluebirds most often build nests of dry grass. Other materials used include woody twigs and pine needles. A few dry leaves, feathers, and where available, a little horsehair may be incorporated. Rarely, a female may use a little moss during nest construction. The base and outer rim of a bluebird nest consist of somewhat coarser material, often lined with finer grasses and rootlets.

A female makes many trips to the nest site carrying nest material. Once inside the cavity or box, she incorporates the new material into the nest. As she works, she may turn around in the nest and press outward with her body to ensure that the nest assumes the appropriate shape. The cups of newly completed bluebird nests usually have an inside diameter of about $2^1/2$ to 3 inches and are about 2 to $2^1/2$ inches deep.

Bluebird nests must provide a suitable environment for the eggs, nestlings, and brooding adult. Temperatures in the nest must be warm, but not too warm, because bluebird eggs and nestlings cannot tolerate temperatures higher than about 107 degrees F. The interior of a cavity or box exposed to full sun on hot days can at times exceed this critical temperature.

The relatively thick walls of many natural cavities provide excellent insulation that keeps temperatures from getting too high. In contrast, the walls of nest boxes are often rather thin, only $1/4$ or $1/2$ inch thick. Such walls provide less effective insulation, and as a result, temperatures inside can sometimes approach or exceed 107 degrees. In general, the thicker the walls and roof of a box, the cooler the inside will be on hot, sunny days. Ventilation from openings in addition to the entrance hole will also help keep the inside of the box cooler.

Although most Eastern Bluebirds are monogamous, in practice, the mating system is more complex, with some individuals using mixed mating strategies. A mixed strategy means forming a pair-bond with one individual but pursuing copulations with other individuals, and for female bluebirds, it can also mean laying eggs in the nests of other pairs (egg dumping). This is one strategy female bluebirds can use when they do not have access to a nest site of their own. A female that loses her nest to a predator during the egg-laying period, before her clutch is complete, can potentially salvage the last egg or two by laying in another pair's nest. As a result, nests sometimes contain eggs and young of mixed parentage. The young bluebirds in a nest may not all have the same genetic father or, if another female has deposited an egg in the nest, the same genetic mother. Young with a different genetic parent or parents are called extrapair young.

The most detailed study of bluebird mating strategies was conducted in South Carolina. In this population, the greater the density of nest boxes, the greater the number of extrapair young. This direct relationship between bluebird density and the number of extrapair young indicates that most such young are fathered by nearby neighbors.

Both male and female bluebirds may actively pursue extrapair copulations by trespassing into the territories of other pairs. Males can benefit from extrapair copulations by producing more young, which in turn will be cared for by other bluebirds. A likely benefit for female bluebirds is greater genetic quality of the young. Females engaging in extrapair copulations with males of better quality than their mates will produce young with better genes. Such young might be healthier and more vigorous, perhaps more resistant to disease and parasites, and may also be able to produce more grandchildren.

For this strategy to work, female bluebirds must be able to discern differences in male quality. Several features of male appearance and behavior, such as the hue and intensity of the blue and rusty plumage, may provide females with such information. Another cue that female bluebirds could use to judge male quality is male singing behavior. Higher-quality males have more time to sing and energy to expend, and sing more song types at higher rates, because such males are better able to compete for resources and are better foragers.

Studies in South Carolina indicate that young males in their first breeding season are more likely to be cuckolded than older males. If female bluebirds perceive older males to be higher-quality males, then the increased number of extrapair young in the nests of younger males indicates that females might be pursuing extrapair copulations to improve the genetic quality of their offspring.

Although some bluebirds pursue mixed mating strategies, most do not. Obviously, it doesn't always pay to pursue extrapair copulations. Any increase in reproductive success achieved by pursuing extrapair copulations must be weighed against possible increases resulting from other activities. For example, a male bluebird pursuing extrapair copulations has less time to feed and defend his own nestlings or fledglings, possibly reducing their chances of survival. The best strategy for many male bluebirds may be to focus on parental efforts rather than extrapair copulations.

Most female bluebirds do not engage in extrapair copulation, presumably because they achieve greater reproductive success or greater genetic quality of young by not participating in such copulations. A female bluebird already paired with a high-quality male would gain little by copulating with other males. In addition, the longer a pair of bluebirds remains together, the greater the likelihood that a female will not engage in extrapair copulations. This suggests that females acquire information about male quality over time and, after a successful nest or two, determine that their mate is of such quality that extrapair copulations would provide little benefit.

Another reason why some females may not participate in extrapair copulations is that males guard their mates, closely following the female during her fertile period. The apparent objective of such guarding is to prevent extrapair copulations. Paired males and females spend more time together during a female's fertile period than either before or after the fertile period, and males are responsible for this association.

If a neighboring female lays an egg in another pair's nest, both members of the pair may invest time and energy in caring for an unrelated offspring. To avoid this, female bluebirds remain closer to their nest sites during egg laying. They also respond aggressively to other female bluebirds, and this aggression is greatest early in the nesting cycle. This suggests that females are responding, at least in part, to the threat of intraspecific brood parasitism, or egg dumping. Such aggression may also serve to protect valuable nest sites.

The function of copulation is to introduce a male's sperm into a female's reproductive tract. In male bluebirds, sperm is produced in the testes. During the nonbreeding period, the testes are very small and do not produce sperm. As spring approaches, the lengthening days stimulate production of hormones that in turn stimulate the testes, which increase dramatically in size. The increasingly large testes produce the hormone testosterone, which stimulates male bluebirds to begin establishing territories and singing.

The reproductive tract of a female bluebird consists of a single ovary (containing several

hundred to a thousand or more eggs) plus an oviduct. The female reproductive tract, under the influence of pituitary hormones, exhibits a tremendous increase in size as the breeding season approaches. The ovary begins to produce the hormone estrogen, which will eventually stimulate females to initiate pair-bonding and other reproductive behaviors. The pituitary also releases increasing amounts of the hormone prolactin, which promotes development of a brood patch and stimulates females to incubate eggs and brood young.

Successful copulations are usually initiated by females. A female bluebird seeking to copulate crouches with her body in a horizontal position and the bill in line with the rest of the body. Her wings droop slightly, with the wing tips held below the base of the tail; feathers on the head and back are compressed; and the tail is usually held upward at a 45-degree angle. With the tail up, the opening into the cloaca—and the female reproductive tract—is exposed. The male then approaches the female from behind or the side and mounts her. The male then brings his cloacal opening into contact with hers in a cloacal kiss. The male ejaculates, releasing several hundred million sperm into the female's cloaca. During copulation, a male bluebird waves his wings to maintain balance on top of the female.

Copulation takes only one to five seconds, and both males and females may give low-volume squeal notes when so engaged. Once deposited in the female's cloaca, sperm begin moving up the oviduct; if no egg is present in the oviduct, some may reach the upper section of the oviduct in fifteen minutes. Not all sperm move up the oviduct; some move into special sperm storage tubules located in the walls of the lower portion of the oviduct. Because sperm may be stored in these tubules for several days and appear to be released continuously, females have a constant supply ready to fertilize eggs.

Copulatory behavior begins a week or even more before a female bluebird lays her first egg and peaks two to five days before egg laying begins. Such timing seems inappropriate, because eggs are available for fertilization during egg laying and not before. However, once a female begins to lay, sperm are unable to make their way up the oviduct because the way is blocked by an egg moving down the oviduct. During egg laying, female bluebirds usually lay one egg every twenty-four hours. As a result, the only time that sperm can move up the oviduct is immediately after an egg has been laid. At this point, ovulation will occur and another egg will enter the oviduct. So for about an hour or less after a female bluebird lays an egg, and

assuming the clutch is not yet complete, introduced sperm have an open pathway up the oviduct. Because male bluebirds may be engaged in other activities, such as defending the territory or chasing away intruding males, and unable to copulate with their mates during that time, the best strategy for the female is to copulate with her mate as much as possible prior to egg laying and get sperm into her storage tubules. Then some of the sperm from those tubules can fertilize the egg.

Bluebird eggs are oval to short-oval. The shell is smooth and glossy, and the basic color is pale blue, bluish white, or, occasionally, pure white. Bluebird eggs are typically about 0.8 by 0.6 inch (21 by 16 millimeters.)

A female bluebird usually begins laying eggs two or three days after completing her nest, but this interval may be anywhere from one to eight days. Eggs are usually laid between one and three hours after sunrise. Although eggs in a clutch are usually laid on successive days, early in the breeding season females occasionally skip a day. Complete clutches usually consist of four or five eggs, although they may range anywhere from two to seven eggs. Clutches are generally smaller later in the breeding season because young produced later in the season are less likely to survive. With less chance of survival, late young are less valuable to adults, and adults put less effort into producing them. Another factor may be the need for adults to begin directing less effort into reproduction and more effort into preparing for migration or the upcoming winter. Particularly in northern areas, adult bluebirds that overextend themselves in a last breeding attempt may be in poorer physical condition as winter approaches and less likely to survive.

Incubation begins after female bluebirds lay the last or, sometimes, the second to last egg of a clutch. When incubating, female bluebirds try to keep the eggs at a temperature of 98 to 100 degrees F, and can do so because they develop a patch of bare, highly vascular skin on the breast called an incubation or brood patch. They also periodically rotate and rearrange the eggs in the nest. This provides for equal heating throughout each egg and also prevents the shell membranes from adhering to the shell, which could interfere with hatching.

Only female bluebirds incubate. Males may enter the nest cavity or box when the female is away, but they rarely sit on the eggs. Even if a male does briefly sit on the eggs, true incubation is not possible, because males have no incubation patch. During the day, female bluebirds alternate incubation periods averaging about fifteen minutes with breaks averaging about ten minutes. Incubation periods are longer, with shorter breaks, during periods of cool weather, and they are shorter during periods of warm weather. While incubating, females preen, stretch, yawn, and for brief periods during the day and longer periods at night, close their eyes and sleep.

During incubation, and even more often during the nestling period, female bluebirds engage in a behavior called tremble-thrusting. A female stands on the rim of the nest, thrusts her bill down into and through the nest, then forcefully and rapidly vibrates her bill against the floor of the cavity or box. Such behavior may help keep the nest clean by shaking nest parasites and other debris to the bottom of the cavity or box. During the nestling period, tremble-thrusting causes the nestlings to shift positions, and this, especially shortly after hatching, may provide all nestlings with equal access to the center—and warmest section—of the nest.

During breaks away from the nest, female bluebirds usually spend most of their time foraging and then, as time permits, resting and preening. When insect prey is abundant and less time must be spent foraging, females spend more time resting and preening.

During incubation, male bluebirds spend much of their time foraging and resting. They also spend time singing and defending the territory as necessary. Males also provide some food for their incubating mates. Females may be fed by males at the nest, but most such feeding occurs away from the nest. When females are incubating, male bluebirds sometimes announce their presence near the nest by calling or singing, and in response, females may fly out to be fed. The food provided by males permits females to spend more time incubating and less time foraging.

Adult bluebirds defend nests with eggs, but the intensity of defense increases dramatically after the young hatch. When a potential predator approaches a nest with eggs, incubating females typically fly from the nest when the predator comes within several feet. Females on nests located in deeper, less vulnerable natural cavities may remain on the eggs, however. A female leaving the nest is often joined by the male, and both may sing or chatter.

During the incubation period, the adults often remain at a distance from the predator while vocalizing. Occasionally, one or both adults may fly closer to, or even dive at, the potential predator, particularly if the intruder is actually at or attempts to enter the nest cavity or box. The intensity of defense by adult bluebirds, as with other birds, is limited during the incubation period because eggs simply aren't as valuable as nestlings. The embryos inside eggs are less likely to survive and eventually reproduce than are nestlings.

Nocturnal predators pose a much greater threat to incubating females. At night, female bluebirds, hesitant to fly in the dark, almost always remain on the nest. Thus if a nocturnal predator, such as a raccoon or black rat snake, raids a nest at night, the incubating female is likely to be killed.

The normal incubation period for Eastern Bluebirds is twelve to fourteen days. As the end of the incubation period approaches, the embryonic bluebird assumes the tucking position, with the bill between the body and the right wing. A day or so before hatching, the young bluebird punctures the innermost shell membrane at the blunt end of the egg with its bill, a process called internal pipping. It then begins to breathe the air between the inner and outer shell membranes. After a few more hours, external pipping begins; the young bluebird breaks through the outer shell, using a hard projection near the tip of its bill called an egg tooth. The young bluebird then continues to peck the shell while slowly rotating; it eventually can penetrate the shell at this circle and begin to emerge from the egg. The entire process from external pipping through hatching may take just an hour or two or, less often, as long as twelve to sixteen hours. Adults usually don't assist the young, although females occasionally help by removing parts of the shell.

Because incubation doesn't begin until the last or next to last egg is laid, all eggs in a clutch normally hatch, in the order of laying, within a few hours of each other, although sometimes the interval between hatching of the first and last eggs may be as long as forty-eight hours. Adults either eat the eggshells or carry the fragments from the nest and dispose of them.

Some eggs do not hatch. Although there is some variation among populations, the percentage of bluebird eggs that fail to hatch is usually less than 7 percent. Eggs may not hatch because one member of a pair is infertile. If so, and assuming genetic monogamy, then the entire clutch would be infertile. Rarely does this occur. More often, just one or two eggs in a clutch of four or five fail to hatch. Such partially infertile clutches might result when sperm fail to fertilize one or more eggs or fertilization occurs but an embryo dies prior to hatching. One factor that might contribute to the death of an embryo is pesticide contamination.

8

Nestlings and Their Parents

At hatching, young bluebirds are naked, blind, and completely dependent on their parents. Newly hatched bluebirds are unable to maintain their body temperatures, so female bluebirds spend much of their time brooding young during the first week after hatching. When brooding, a female places her brood patch against nestlings to facilitate the transfer of heat. Young bluebirds begin to regulate their own body temperatures when about a week old, and the time spent brooding by female bluebirds then begins to decline. If the weather is cooler than usual, however, females will continue to spend much of their time brooding. By the time young are ten to thirteen days old, females no longer brood during the day but may continue brooding at night for a few more days.

Nestlings need lots of food. A bluebird nestling that fledges when twenty days old may have been fed nine hundred times! Some simple math reveals that adult bluebirds make thousands of trips to the nest with food when raising broods of four or five young. Males and females usually contribute equally to the provisioning of the nestlings. The extent of each adult's contribution may, however, vary with the age of nestlings. Typically, provisioning rates of male bluebirds decline somewhat as the nestling period progresses, while female provisioning rates tend to increase.

Studies in which male bluebirds have been temporarily removed during the nestling period indicate that females are able to compensate by increasing their provisioning rates. As a result, nestlings of female bluebirds without mates grow at the same rates and are as likely to fledge as those of females being assisted by males. If, as this study suggests, their assistance is not essential, then why do male bluebirds feed nestlings? Possibly because male provisioning permits females to conserve energy in preparation for another nesting attempt.

Bluebirds sometimes lose their mates due to predation during the incubation or nestling period. A male bluebird that loses a mate during incubation cannot assume incubation duties because males have no brood patch. The nest is necessarily abandoned, and unless it's late in the breeding season, the male attempts to attract a new mate. Female bluebirds that lose their mates during incubation sometimes desert the nest, but they often continue to incubate and attempt to raise the young unaided. Both male and female bluebirds that lose a mate during the nestling period typically attempt to raise their young unaided and often are successful.

Some adult bluebirds that lose mates during the incubation or nestling period are able to obtain new mates. These new mates are usually floaters—unpaired, nonterritorial individuals that range, often unnoticed, throughout the territories of several pairs in search of food and other resources. Floaters have been reported in many species of birds, including bluebirds, even though floating would seem to be a poor strategy because, with no mate or territory, successful reproduction is obviously impossible. However, when resources such as nest sites or good-quality territories are in short supply, floating may be the only option for some individuals.

When a male or female bluebird obtains such a replacement mate during the incubation or nestling period, the replacement mate usually provides little or no parental care. A replacement female will not incubate a clutch of eggs laid by a male bluebird's previous mate. Occasionally such a replacement mate will feed the nestlings, but if so, it is at a low rate.

The tendency for replacement mates to provide little assistance in raising young is not surprising. The parental behavior of birds is greatly influenced by hormones, and nonbreeding floaters that become replacement mates may be physiologically incapable of exhibiting such behavior. In addition, investing substantial effort in caring for unrelated young would provide little or no benefit to the foster parent, as its genes are not represented in these offspring.

However, becoming a replacement mate, and even providing a little parental care for the other bird's offspring, may pay off in future breeding opportunities, because replacement mates obtain a breeding territory and a potential future mate. A bluebird that becomes a replacement mate may be able to help its new mate in another nesting attempt later in the current breeding season and perhaps in future years.

Most bluebirds do make it through the breeding period without losing their mates. Even so, male bluebirds may not be the genetic fathers of all their nestlings, because their mates may have engaged in extrapair copulations. There is no evidence, however, that males or females of any bird species can tell which nestlings are theirs in a genetic sense, and parents typically care for all nestlings equally.

Over an entire nestling period, adult bluebirds typically average about five or six feeding trips to the nest per hour. Feeding rates are lower during the first day or two after hatching, then increase and may remain relatively constant, or perhaps increase slightly, until the young are about sixteen or seventeen days old. Thereafter, and until the young fledge, usually at eighteen to twenty-one days, adults make fewer visits to the nest.

During the first few days after hatching, female bluebirds spend much of their time brooding. Males bring in most of the food during this time, often giving it to the brooding female, who in turn feeds the nestlings. If the nestlings are not hungry, the female will consume the food delivered by the male. Such feeding of the female reduces the amount of time she must spend foraging and permits her to spend more time brooding. If the female is off the nest, males provide food directly to the young.

When feeding nestlings, adults prefer to forage near the nest. Traveling to more distant sites requires more energy, and when farther from the nest, they are less likely to spot predators approaching the nest. For most pairs, most foraging occurs within 500 feet of the nest. But the birds must forage where sufficient food can be obtained, and foraging sites can be substantial distances from the nest. Because it does require more time and energy to travel to sites farther from the nest, adult bluebirds foraging at such sites typically spend more time at the site and often return to the nest with larger loads, carrying more or larger prey items.

Older, larger nestlings require more food to supply sufficient energy for temperature maintenance and additional growth. Adult songbirds often increase feeding rates to meet the increasing demands of older nestlings. This is true of bluebirds, which usually make more

visits to the nest and sometimes bring larger prey or more prey items per visit. This trend does not continue through the entire nestling period, however. Young bluebirds don't eat as much as the time of fledging approaches, so beginning several days before fledging, the number of visits to the nest by adult bluebirds levels off and may even decline. The young bluebirds' loss of appetite translates into a decline in weight just before fledging; this lighter weight is likely beneficial as they learn to fly.

Brood size has little effect on provisioning rates. Adult bluebirds at nests with three, four, or even five young make about the same number of feeding trips. This means that individual nestlings in large broods receive less food than those in smaller broods. Despite this, nestling bluebirds in larger broods grow at the same rate as those in smaller broods; they require less food than those in smaller broods because the amount of energy they need to maintain normal body temperature is lower. Nestlings huddled together in a nest can share body heat, and each nestling has less exposed body surface.

Nestling bluebirds are fed many different insects, including butterfly and moth larvae (caterpillars), grasshoppers, crickets, katydids, spiders, beetles, and earthworms. Adults bring newly hatched young more small, soft-bodied prey, such as spiders and caterpillars. Prey items fed to nestlings during the first few days after hatching are usually no longer than about $2/3$ inch long, an appropriate size—but still quite a mouthful—for young only $1^1/2$ to 2 inches long themselves. Soft-bodied spiders and caterpillars are easier to digest than hard-bodied prey like grasshoppers or beetles and may contain nutrients needed by very young birds. With increasing age, the nestlings' digestive systems become more efficient, and they can eat more hard-bodied insect prey.

As the young birds grow larger, the average size of the food items delivered by adults also increases. Several days after hatching, when young bluebirds begin to receive more large, hard-bodied prey like grasshoppers and crickets from parents, adults sometimes make the insects easier for them to swallow and digest by battering the prey items against a perch to remove legs and wings and crushing the insects in their bills before giving them to their young.

Young bluebirds solicit food from their parents by begging. When begging, nestling bluebirds call and simultaneously extend their heads upward with mouths wide open. In very young nestlings, any movement of the nest stimulates begging. As they grow older, nestlings learn to ignore incidental movements and respond only to the vocalizations or presence of their parents. Studies of other songbird nestlings indicate that the nestling that starts to beg first, reaches highest, and holds its beak closest to the parent is the most likely to be fed. In other words, adults in most species do not keep track of which nestlings they feed, nor do they make sure that all the young receive similar amounts of food. Most adult songbirds simply feed the nestling that begs most vigorously. Typically, begging intensity is related to a nestling's hunger level, increasing as the time since last being fed increases. Thus nestlings fed most recently tend to beg less vigorously, and as a result, all nestlings usually receive similar amounts of food from their parents. Although nestlings do compete indirectly, each doing its best to obtain food from parents visiting the nest, there is no direct aggression among siblings.

Although most adult birds simply feed the nestling that begs most vigorously, some species, including Eastern Bluebirds, exhibit sex-biased provisioning, with nestlings of one sex receiving more food. Male bluebirds tend to provide more food for daughters than for sons, perhaps because sons represent potential competitors. Young female bluebirds tend to disperse farther from parental territories than young males, and as a result, females are unlikely to compete with parents for resources. Young males, on the other hand, usually remain closer to parental territories and may, in the future, compete with their fathers for resources, including mates.

Although nestling bluebirds utter begging calls, especially when a parent arrives at the nest, the calls themselves have little to do with determining which nestling will be fed. They do, however, serve an important function. In a study of Great Tits in Europe, adults increased their feeding rates when recorded begging calls were played over speakers near the nests. The relationship between nestling begging calls and adult provisioning rates has also been tested, in a somewhat different manner, in Eastern Bluebirds. After being abandoned by their parents for unknown reasons, four fifteen-day-old young were transferred to a nest already containing five young about the same age. The abandoned nestlings had not been fed for some time, and as a result, they begged incessantly. The adult bluebirds at this nest, upon hearing begging calls being uttered by their newly enlarged brood of nine nestlings, responded by making forty trips to the nest in the next hour.

Such observations suggest that nestlings could entice adults into providing more food simply by begging with greater intensity. Several studies have revealed, however, that nestling birds do not do so. Nestlings beg vigorously when hungry, but once satiated, they beg less vigorously or not at all. Thus adult songbirds can use the nestlings' collective vocalizing to assess their hunger level and adjust feeding rates accordingly. Adults bring enough food to ensure that their young continue to grow as they should but do not bring more food than is necessary.

Another parental duty is to dispose of the nestling bluebirds' fecal material. Nest sanitation is important. A nest must be kept dry and warm to maintain its insulating capacity. The bacteria and parasites that would thrive in an accumulation of fecal material could harm the nestlings, causing illness or even death. The odor of accumulated fecal material might attract potential nest predators. The fecal material of songbird nestlings is enclosed in a tough mucous membrane, forming what is called a fecal sac; this makes cleanup easier for the adults.

During the first five days after hatching, adult bluebirds eat most of the fecal sacs produced by nestlings. Thereafter, progressively fewer fecal sacs are eaten. Adults sometimes eat fecal sacs produced by six- to nine-day-old nestlings but rarely eat those of ten-day-old or older nestlings. Fecal sacs not consumed by adults are carried at least 50 feet from the nest and are either dropped or deposited on a perch.

At hatching, young bluebirds weigh about 0.09 ounce (2.5 grams), or 8 percent of an average adult's weight. Thereafter, nestling bluebirds gain weight at an average rate of about 0.07 to 0.09 ounce per day until about twelve days old. Nestling weight then fluctuates but remains relatively constant until fledging. Some of the food provided by the parents is used to generate new tissue, but some must also be used for respiration and other body functions, such as the production of body heat. In addition, some energy is used for muscle contraction. Throughout the nestling period, small birds like nestling bluebirds use about 20 percent of the energy gained from parental feeding for growth, 60 percent for respiration and maintenance, and 20 percent for activity. As the end of the nestling period approaches, young bluebirds usually weigh about 0.9 to 1 ounce (26 to 28 grams), which is about 90 percent of the typical adult weight of about 1.1 ounces (30 grams).

At hatching, young bluebirds are mostly pinkish red, with just a few scattered tufts of grayish down in the feather tracts from which feathers will later emerge. The future flight and tail feathers are barely noticeable as tiny dark spots. Newly hatched young have protruding abdomens and large eyes covered with dark lids. Their legs and wings are very small. Because muscles are still weak, their heads wobble slightly as they beg. In many species, the mouths of nestlings are brightly colored and have special markings that aid adults in placing food items in the proper position. Nestling bluebirds have yellow or yellow-red mouths with bright, yellowish white margins. These light-colored margins help adult bluebirds accurately deliver food into the mouths of their young, even in a dark cavity or nest box.

Not all body structures develop at the same rate. Those used most by nestling bluebirds develop the most quickly. The mouth is of obvious importance, and gape width and bill length increase rapidly during the first several days after hatching. This allows older nestlings, with increasing energy needs, to handle larger food items. Wings, which are not used until fledging, develop more slowly.

As the nestlings develop, their eyes gradually open, beginning about five or six days after hatching, and their juvenal plumage begins to develop. By seventeen days, young bluebirds are completely covered with feathers, and only a few scattered tufts of down remain.

During their first four or five days, nestling bluebirds are brooded much of the time and do very little beyond raising their heads and gaping when an adult arrives at the nest with food. Although levels of activity do increase somewhat with increasing age, nestlings at all stages spend most of their time simply resting and growing. By twelve days after hatching, nestlings exhibit better muscular coordination and begin preening their feathers, exercising their wings, and orienting toward their parents when they arrive at the nest. At about the same age, the sex of nestlings can be determined by examining the wing feathers. Young males have bright blue wings, whereas those of females are paler gray-blue. By seventeen or eighteen days, young bluebirds begin looking out of the cavity or nest box; they usually leave the nest eighteen to twenty days after hatching.

Among songbirds, the duration of the nestling period is influenced by size and nest location. Larger species have longer nestling periods, and species like bluebirds that nest in cavities or boxes have longer nestling periods than open-cup nesters. Open-cup nests are at higher risk of nest predation, so it's beneficial for young to leave such nests as soon as possible.

Before they can survive outside of the nest, nestlings must achieve a particular level of maturation or development. A nestling that leaves the nest before it is able to maintain its body temperature or has sufficient muscular control to maintain its position on a perch is not likely to survive. Once that level of development has been reached, hunger and sibling competition are probably what induce young bluebirds to leave the nest. A nestling probably leaves the nest in an attempt to approach its parents and obtain additional feedings at the expense of its siblings. Once one nestling has left the nest, parents may preferentially feed that nestling. Siblings remaining in the nest are not fed at all, or at least not as frequently. This stimulates them to follow their newly fledged sibling.

9

Fledging and the Postfledging Period

For several days before nest departure, young bluebirds are very active and spend much time preening and exercising their wings. Older nestlings also spend time at the entrance and, perhaps to get a better view, sometimes extend their heads and upper bodies out of the entrance. Eventually a young bluebird may lean out so far that returning to the cavity or box would be difficult, if not impossible. At that point, or within a minute or two, fledging occurs. Once the first young bluebird has departed the nest, the others generally follow over the next hour or two. Occasionally, fledging of an entire brood takes most of a day or, rarely, two. Nestlings often leave the nest in the morning but may do so at any time of the day. The time of nest departure is usually determined by the young bluebirds. However, adults are sometimes observed calling in an apparent attempt to induce fledging, particularly when a potential predator, such as a human, is near the nest. Although fledging normally occurs when young bluebirds are eighteen to twenty days old, disturbance of a nest with young at least fourteen days old may cause premature fledging.

Young bluebirds that fledge when eighteen to twenty days old typically fly—slowly at first, then faster—somewhere between 15 to 60 feet to their first perch. Those that fledge prematurely can't fly as well or as far and may have to spend a day or two on the ground near the nest. Young bluebirds on their first flight often land awkwardly and sometimes miss the intended perch and flutter to the ground. Smooth landings may be a problem for fledglings for several days after leaving the nest, because their tail feathers, or rectrices, are not fully developed. Newly fledged young may make several short flights before finding a suitable perch, preferably one that is relatively high, sheltered, and next to a tree trunk.

As young fledge, adults remain nearby and sometimes even accompany fledglings on their first flight. Adults respond vigorously to the presence of potential predators, uttering chatter calls and even flying or diving at crows, Blue Jays, Common Grackles, humans, and any other perceived threat. Parents continue to feed their young after fledging, and fledglings may be fed more often than siblings still in the nest cavity or box. Food offered to but not taken by satiated fledglings may then be taken to the nestlings.

At fledging, young bluebirds have not yet attained adult size, and will not do so until about thirty-five to forty days old, or two to three weeks after fledging. Newly fledged bluebirds weigh about 90 percent of adult weight. Adult wing chords, from the "wrist" to the tip of the longest primary, average about 4 inches (100 millimeters), while those of recent fledglings average about $2^{3}/_{4}$ inches (72 millimeters). Adult tails are about 2.4 to 2.6 inches (60 to 65 millimeters) long, while those of newly fledged young are only about 1.2 to 1.6 inches (35 to 40 millimeters) long.

After fledging, the main flight feathers (primaries and secondaries) and the tail feathers (rectrices) of young bluebirds continue to grow. Within a week to ten days, the flight feathers have completed their growth. The tail feathers grow more slowly and may not complete development until about three weeks after fledging.

Fledglings differ from adults in appearance, having brownish spots on their breasts. This plumage helps fledglings blend in with their surroundings, particularly when perched among tree limbs. Because recently fledged bluebirds are easy prey, good camouflage is important. When they detect a potential predator or are alerted by the whine or chatter calls of their parents, fledglings remain motionless, with their beaks pointed slightly upward. Only if a predator comes very close will a recently fledged bluebird take flight. Older fledglings are more likely to take flight upon the approach of a predator, particularly one approaching on the ground.

When about two months old, young male and female bluebirds begin a molt that typically lasts five to ten weeks. During this molt, called the first prebasic molt, all feathers are lost except the primaries (plus the tenth primary covert), the secondaries, and, for subspecies in Central America and young from late nests in more northern populations, the tail feathers. With the completion of this molt, the plumage of young bluebirds now resembles that of adults and is called the first basic plumage.

Siblings usually roost together once all have fledged, and at least one adult is almost always nearby. Typically, family groups remain near the nest site for several days after the young fledge. With increasing age, young bluebirds are much better at flying and landing, and by three to five days postfledging, they begin to follow their parents. At this point, family groups may leave the vicinity of the nest, as sites that provide good foraging and cover for fledglings may be some distance from the nest site.

Fledgling bluebirds spend much of their time resting and sleeping. Periods of rest are typically fifteen to sixty minutes long. When they are over, fledglings often begin to utter begging calls, which permit adults to quickly locate and feed fledglings. To alert young to their presence, approaching adults may utter *tu-a-wee* calls. In addition to vocalizing, fledglings initiate a begging display, with the head drawn back between the wings, legs flexed and body lowered. The begging fledgling gapes, fluffs its feathers, and wing-quivers, lifting and extending its wings while moving them rapidly up and down. The intensity of the fledgling's begging display increases as an adult gets closer and peaks just before the young bird is fed. As the adult departs, the fledgling continues to beg, but the intensity of the display gradually diminishes. After being fed several times, and as hunger levels decline, fledglings call and display with reduced vigor and may simply wing-quiver without uttering any calls. Between feedings, fledglings are usually quiet, although if they are still hungry, they may continue to utter begging calls, but at a lower rate and volume than when adults are nearby.

The diet of fledglings is like that of nestlings—almost entirely insects. Because fledglings, especially recent ones, are usually in trees, adult bluebirds may spend more time foraging on nearby branches and leaves and less time from perches near the ground.

Young bluebirds may make their first attempts at foraging for themselves just a few days after fledging. Initially, perched young may try to capture small insect prey on nearby branches or leaves. By seven to ten days after fledging, young bluebirds may make their first attempts at capturing prey on the ground. Although some aspects of foraging, such as beating prey on a branch after capture, are likely innate, much learning is also involved. For example, fledglings must learn where they can and cannot perch. Young bluebirds often find that what may appear to be suitable perches, such as grasses and various herbs, cannot support their weight. Fledglings also learn to hold insects by the head or thorax so they can't escape and to remove the appendages from large insects like crickets and grasshoppers. Some learning is by trial and error, but young may also learn by watching parents and siblings.

By two to two and a half weeks after fledging, the hunting skills of young bluebirds are improving, but it's likely that, on average, only about one-third of their capture attempts are successful. Adult bluebirds, in contrast, probably succeed at least twice as often. Because of their limited hunting success, fledglings still spend time following and being fed by their parents, but they also begin to move throughout the territory—and into adjacent territories—on their own. Learning to forage efficiently takes several months, and even after becoming independent, young bluebirds do not forage as well as adults. This no doubt contributes to the high mortality rates during their first winter.

Young bluebirds are usually independent of their parents about three to four weeks after leaving the nest. Young that fledge early in the breeding season may become independent earlier than those that fledge from later nests, because parents that renest are engaged in other activities. Later in the season, adults will not renest and may care for fledglings longer.

Bluebird pairs usually renest after a successful first nesting attempt. A typical interval between the fledging of a brood and the laying of the first egg of the next nest is three weeks, although this depends on the number of fledglings. A pair with fewer fledglings to care for may initiate their next nest several days sooner than pairs with more fledglings. Adult females may continue to feed fledglings, at decreasing rates, until the first egg of her next nest is laid. By this time, the fledglings are becoming increasingly independent, and the adult male alone can now care for them. In fact, because nearly independent fledglings require much less care than younger fledglings, adult male bluebirds now have less to do. Observations of adult males with older fledglings at least ten days postfledging reveal that they may spend as much as one-third of their time resting, compared with just 10 to 15 percent during the nestling period.

All young bluebirds eventually leave parental territories and move to another location. The timing of this movement, called natal dispersal, is likely influenced by several factors. As the postfledging period progresses, young bluebirds receive less food from parents and must obtain more themselves. Because they are not yet accomplished foragers, young may not get as much food during this time, and this causes physiological stress. Additional stress may be created if adult bluebirds respond aggressively to begging by fledglings or to the presence of fledglings near their next nest. In response, the adrenal glands of young bluebirds increase production of a hormone called corticosterone. This hormone stimulates the young birds to become more active, which may lead them to depart from parental territories. Young bluebirds in good physical condition may disperse soon after corticosterone levels begin to increase. Other young may increase their foraging activity, which may cause them to gain weight and may improve their condition. Then these young may also disperse from parental territories.

Young bluebirds exhibit much variation in the timing of this departure from parental territories, and some may have not yet left when their renesting parents again begin feeding nestlings. Occasionally, fledglings from a previous nest assist parents in feeding these nestlings. The food provided by fledgling helpers is not essential, and the extra activity at the nest could even be detrimental if it alerted a predator to the presence of an active nest. Perhaps the main benefit to helping is that young bluebirds gain valuable experience, which may improve their chances of successful reproduction in subsequent breeding seasons.

In general, young bluebirds disperse relatively short distances. A study in South Carolina revealed that the territories of young bluebirds breeding for the first time were an average of 0.8 mile (1.25 kilometers) from parental territories. Young males dispersed shorter distances than young females, with an average distance of 0.7 mile (1.08 kilometers) for males and 0.9 mile (1.39 kilometers) for females.

For young bluebirds in southern areas, natal dispersal may represent a relatively direct movement. For young in northern populations, natal dispersal is not direct. These young bluebirds must first migrate to wintering areas, then return to breeding territories. The location of a young bird's first breeding territory relative to that of its parents' territory represents the natal dispersal distance.

Natal dispersal poses potential risks. Young birds moving through unfamiliar areas may be particularly vulnerable to predation. It also provides benefits. Moving away from parents and siblings decreases the chances of inbreeding and may increase opportunities for obtaining resources such as a breeding territory or mate.

In many species of birds, including bluebirds, young females tend to disperse farther than young males. The reasons for such sex-biased dispersal are not completely understood. The mating system of bluebirds may be one important factor. Male bluebirds establish breeding territories that contain resources essential to successful reproduction, and females may choose mates based, at least in part, on the quality of these territories. Young males remaining near their natal territories may be more likely to establish good-quality territories because familiarity with an area may permit higher feeding rates and lower predation rates.

During and after dispersal, young bluebirds form flocks consisting of sibling groups from one or more broods. Flocks may consist of two to ten or more juveniles but typically contain about six young bluebirds. Young bluebirds in these flocks sometimes chase and supplant each other, assuming the perch of the other bird. Juveniles occasionally engage in reproductive activities, with young females sometimes pecking at or briefly carrying dried grass or other nesting material, and young males attempting to copulate with females in the flock. Young of both sexes regularly inspect cavities. These activities provide young bluebirds with important experience that will no doubt prove useful in the future.

By way of chases, supplanting behavior, and less frequently, actual fighting, young bluebirds in these flocks develop complex dominance relationships. In some bird species, individuals in flocks develop straight-line dominance hierarchies, with individual A dominant over B, B over C, and so on. In flocks of young bluebirds, relationships are more complicated. For example, bluebird A may be dominant over B, and B over C, but C then dominates A. Reversals can occur: A may almost always dominate B, but occasionally, B dominates A. Factors that determine dominance status in bluebird flocks are unclear but may include age and size. Dominant bluebirds benefit by gaining access to important resources, such as foraging and roosting sites.

Flocks of young bluebirds form in the summer and may persist for several weeks or months. During the fall and winter, flocks include adults as well. In northern areas, flocks of migrating bluebirds form; farther south, winter flocks may consist of both juveniles and adults, some of which are residents and others migrants.

Prior to migration in the north, and during the fall and winter farther south, juvenile bluebirds in roving flocks no doubt evaluate areas as potential territories. As flocks move through different areas, juveniles acquire information concerning the availability of cavities and other resources. Such information will be important the following spring, when young bluebirds attempt to breed for the first time.

First-year birds, especially small songbirds, typically suffer high mortality rates, and it's likely that about 60 to 70 percent of young bluebirds die during their first year of life. During the nestling period and shortly after fledging, high mortality rates are due primarily to predation. Another period of high mortality probably occurs immediately after parents stop feeding fledglings. Studies of other species have found that newly independent young birds usually lose weight because they forage less efficiently than adults. If young bluebirds become proficient enough at foraging to survive the first two to three weeks of independence, their chances of surviving until the next breeding season improve dramatically. Predators such as Sharp-shinned and Cooper's Hawks will continue to take some young bluebirds throughout the winter, and some, particularly in harsh winters, may die of starvation, but after the first weeks of juvenile independence, mortality rates for first-year bluebirds probably decline and approach those of adults. Even for adult bluebirds, however, mortality rates are probably about 40 to 50 percent. Thus most bluebirds live for only a year or two; few live for more than four or five years.

The Nonbreeding Period

As the end of the breeding season approaches, adult Eastern Bluebirds begin to molt, and old feathers are replaced with new ones. Caring for young and molting take substantial amounts of energy, and minimizing overlap between these two activities would seem to be beneficial. Nevertheless, particularly in the northern parts of their range, adults must initiate molt before their young are independent so that molt will be complete in time for migration. When parental care and molting overlap, bluebirds need plenty of energy. Fortunately, insects and fruit are usually abundant at this time of year.

Most bluebirds complete their molt by sometime in September. Adults with young generally take longer and may not complete their molt until early October. The molt of feathers needed for flight is gradual, taking about seven weeks, so bluebirds are always able to fly. The energy cost of replacing feathers is related to their size. Those that cost the most, therefore, are the flight feathers and tail feathers. So that the cost will not be too great at any given time, molt of the tail feathers begins only after most flight feathers have been replaced.

After molt is complete, Eastern Bluebirds actually look a bit duller and not, as might be expected, brighter and more colorful. This is because the new body feathers—though not the flight and tail feathers—have brownish tips. These tips are gradually worn off during the winter, and as the next breeding season approaches, bluebirds, especially males, are again a brighter blue.

By September, many bluebirds can be found in flocks. Some flocks consist largely or entirely of juveniles from earlier nests. Other flocks may be family units, consisting of a pair plus young from their last nest. These family flocks may then join to form larger flocks. Flocks occasionally consist of one hundred or more bluebirds but more typically include three to twenty. In southern areas (roughly south of the Ohio River), most bluebirds in these flocks are residents. In northern populations, juvenile and family flocks, or at least most flock members, begin migrating south in late September and October.

As is true for other migratory species of birds, the timing of migration by bluebirds appears to be determined largely by photoperiod. At the time of departure, weather conditions usually are still reasonably pleasant and food is still available. Weather can have an influence on migration, however. Mild weather may induce migrating bluebirds to linger longer at sites where they have stopped to forage and rest. And inclement weather may cause them to move south at a faster pace.

As the days grow shorter, bluebirds become more active or restless, probably because of increased production of corticosterone by the adrenal glands. As a result, bluebirds begin their southward movement. Little is known about this movement, but bluebirds probably move to their wintering grounds over a period of several days or even weeks, depending on the distance traveled, and when migrating, they travel during the day. Bluebirds may spend a day or more at favorable locations, such as particularly good foraging areas, before resuming migration. Migrating bluebirds may also temporarily join resident flocks. As residents are familiar with the area, following them may help the migrants find food, water, and roost sites.

During fall migration, Eastern Bluebirds travel in a southerly direction, sometimes almost due south, but other times more to the southeast or southwest. Bluebirds may use a solar compass to determine which way is south. This seems likely, because many other species of birds are known to use the position of the sun as a compass. To consistently orient in a particular direction, a bluebird would have to compensate for the sun's movement across the sky, because the position of the sun relative to any point changes continuously by 15 degrees per hour. Other species of birds do this, and bluebirds are likely to have this ability as well. Because flocks consisting entirely of inexperienced, juvenile bluebirds migrate south, some innate or intrinsic mechanism must be used for orientation, and the sun compass seems likely.

Evidence suggests that many Eastern Bluebirds that breed in Canada and the northern United States exhibit leapfrog migration. In other words, bluebirds do not simply shift south, with northern bluebirds moving south into areas vacated by bluebirds that moved farther south. Rather, many northern bluebirds leapfrog over areas occupied by many resident bluebirds, continuing through the Carolinas, Kentucky, Tennessee, and Missouri to Louisiana, Mississippi, Florida, and the southern portions of Alabama, Georgia, and Texas. Similar behavior has been reported for a few other species of birds, including Fox Sparrows.

One likely reason for leapfrog migration is that these northern bluebirds migrate through areas with the highest densities of resident bluebirds—Missouri, eastern Oklahoma, Kentucky, Tennessee, the Carolinas, northern Alabama and Georgia, and northeast Texas—and continue on to areas with fewer residents, which likely means less competition. Wintering farther south may also mean milder weather and more food, at least more insects.

Not all northern bluebirds exhibit this migration pattern. Some move shorter distances and winter in areas with greater numbers of resident bluebirds. Those doing so may face greater competition for resources but benefit by remaining closer to their breeding grounds. If they survive, these bluebirds are likely to be among the first to return to more northern breeding areas in the spring.

Most migrating bluebirds arrive on wintering grounds sometime between late September and November. The arrival of these winter visitors can greatly increase the bluebird populations in southern states. In some parts of Florida, for example, bluebird populations may increase by more than 100 percent during the winter.

Although most bluebirds that breed in Canada and the northern United States move south for the winter, a few do not. Some bluebirds attempt to overwinter as far north as Massachusetts, southern New York, southern Ontario, southern Michigan, southern Wisconsin, and Iowa. These birds represent only a small percentage (perhaps 2 to 10 percent) of the breeding populations in these areas, however, and there does not appear to be a correlation between the number of nonmigratory bluebirds in these northern areas and weather conditions. If more bluebirds are observed in these areas during mild winters, it may not mean that fewer migrated but that more nonmigratory bluebirds survive such winters. The apparent absence of any correlation between the tendency to migrate and weather suggests that migration by Eastern Bluebirds has a genetic basis, with some bluebirds programmed to migrate and others not. The number of bluebirds so programmed increases with increasing latitude; most northern bluebirds migrate, but most southern bluebirds do not.

Eastern Bluebirds, both migrants and residents, generally use the same types of habitats during the nonbreeding season as during the breeding season. One difference, particularly farther south, is that cavities or nest boxes are not an essential component of winter ranges. During the nonbreeding season, bluebirds spend much of their time foraging but, depending on weather conditions, also have time to rest and preen.

Eastern Bluebirds eat more fruit during the nonbreeding season, with the importance of fruit as a food source increasing as latitude increases. If fruit supplies are depleted or covered with ice, bluebirds in the area may die. Although surviving northern winters may be difficult, bluebirds that do so benefit by having first access to breeding areas in the spring.

As during migration, bluebirds are typically found in flocks during the winter. Being part of a flock may have some disadvantages, including increased competition for resources such as food or roost sites. The outcome of such competition may depend on a bluebird's status within the flock, with more dominant individuals having better access to resources than lower-ranking birds.

But flocks also provide some important advantages. A bluebird in a flock is less likely to be killed by a predator, as more individuals are watching and will usually spot an approaching predator sooner than could a lone bird. Individual bluebirds in a flock are also able to spend less time scanning for potential predators, because other flock members are scanning as well. Also, a bluebird in a flock might be able to more easily locate food or good foraging sites by watching other flock members.

During the nonbreeding period, bluebirds are sometimes found in the vicinity of other species, including Field and White-throated Sparrows, Pine Warblers, Dark-eyed Juncos, American Robins, and Cedar Waxwings. Such temporary associations result when bluebirds and other species are attracted to the same location by a needed resource such as food or roost sites. Although these associations might provide some limited benefit, such as improved predator detection, they can also create competition. Other fruit-eating birds, such as American Robins, European Starlings, and, especially, Northern Mockingbirds, may chase bluebirds from a fruit source.

Conserving energy can be extremely important for bluebirds, particularly during cold weather. Bluebirds, like other birds, are endothermic, or warm-blooded, and maintain a body temperature of about 105 degrees F (41 degrees C). Maintaining this temperature requires energy, and the amount of energy needed changes with the ambient temperature. During the winter months, bluebirds can control body temperature by changing feather position, fluffing up feathers as temperatures decline, and by changing patterns of blood flow, directing blood away from the body surface and, especially, the legs and feet so less heat is lost. During cold weather, bluebirds must also generate more heat and use more energy. As temperatures get cooler, bluebirds first tense their muscles, especially those in their breasts and legs, and begin to shiver. This muscular activity creates heat but also uses energy. The colder the temperatures, the more energy bluebirds must use to stay warm. Finding and staying in microclimates that provide slightly warmer temperatures and protection from the elements, such as wind, can help a bluebird conserve substantial amounts of energy.

Bluebirds spend some time roosting during the day, and selecting a site that provides protection from potential predators and the elements is important. Selecting a good nocturnal roost site is even more important, because more time is spent at these roosts, and temperatures are lower at night. Bluebirds often spend the night in trees that provide both concealment and a favorable microclimate, such as pines and cedars. They also use deciduous trees that retain at least some leaves during the fall and winter, such as some oaks.

Most bluebirds appear to prefer open roost sites, but during cold weather, they will roost in cavities. Normally, only one bluebird occupies a particular roost cavity. During especially cold weather, however, flocks of bluebirds may roost communally. Reports of such communal roosts indicate that anywhere from two to twenty bluebirds may use a single cavity or box and that these bluebirds tend to roost with all heads oriented toward the center of the cavity or box. This position, when there are several bluebirds present, minimizes the risk of suffocation and maximizes body contact, which reduces the amount of energy required to stay warm. During long, cold nights, saving energy may save a bluebird's life.

Eastern Bluebirds also can save energy during cold nights by lowering their body temperature. Normally, a bluebird's body temperature is about 105 degrees F. Most nights, a bluebird's body temperature probably drops a few degrees. On very cold nights, a bluebird may lower its temperature by as much as 10 to 15 degrees, a condition referred to as nocturnal hypothermia. The body's metabolism, including the heart rate and respiration rate, is slowed down, thereby saving energy, and the decreased contrast between body temperature and air temperature reduces heat loss and also saves energy. Entering and recovering from this hypothermia takes time, so during very cold weather, bluebirds may arrive at roost sites earlier and leave later than usual. When hypothermic, bluebirds are less responsive. As they recover, they may be a bit sluggish when first leaving roosts in the morning.

Despite their behavioral and physiological adaptations for coping with winter, many Eastern Bluebirds do not survive. Mortality rates vary with location and weather. During extended periods of cold, snowy weather, foraging may be more difficult, and the combination of reduced food intake and increased energy needs can lead to starvation. Such mortality has been documented on many occasions and in many areas. Ice storms can be particularly devastating for bluebirds. A layer of ice covering the ground and fruit makes foraging nearly impossible, and if the ice persists for several days, many bluebirds may perish.

Occasionally, severe conditions with below-normal temperatures along with snow and ice persist over a good portion of the Eastern Bluebird's winter range. The winters of 1976–1977 and 1977–1978 were unusually severe, and the extended cold during these winters throughout much of the bluebird's range caused high mortality and extreme declines in bluebird populations.

Eastern Bluebirds also face other hazards during the nonbreeding season. A variety of predators including the accipiters, or bird-eating hawks, sometimes prey on bluebirds. Both Cooper's and Sharp-shinned Hawks prey primarily on songbirds, including bluebirds. Another predator that occasionally preys on bluebirds is the Eastern Screech-Owl. Screech-owls are nocturnal and may take bluebirds from their nighttime roosts. These owls sometimes become active before sunset and probably observe birds as they go to their roosts.

As days begin to lengthen during January and February, migrant Eastern Bluebirds once again become more active or restless and begin their northward migration. The speed of this northward movement appears to be influenced by weather—specifically, the temperature—to a greater degree than that of the southward movement in the fall. As the line representing above-freezing mean temperatures gradually moves northward in early spring, the earliest migrating bluebirds follow. As a result, bluebirds are often among the first migrants to appear on breeding areas in the spring, usually arriving in northern states and southern Canada in early to mid-March. Adults arrive on breeding areas before juveniles, and adult males are often the first to arrive in northern breeding areas. Many males, however, arrive at breeding sites with females.

Some adult Eastern Bluebirds return to the same breeding sites used the previous year; others move to new ones. Reproductive failure is the primary reason for this movement to a new breeding site, which is called breeding dispersal. At one location in South Carolina, for example, 56 percent of bluebirds that successfully raised young returned to the same site the next year. In contrast, only 15 percent of unsuccessful bluebirds returned to the same breeding site.

Relations with Humans

The lives of Eastern Bluebirds, like the lives of so many other animals, have been affected by humans. The introduction of House Sparrows and European Starlings into North America shows how humans can create problems for a native species. But human activities affect bluebirds in many other ways as well.

An estimated 57 million birds, including many bluebirds, are killed by vehicles in the United States each year. Bluebirds also die from exposure to pesticides, the use of which is widespread in the United States, with over 1 billion pounds used each year. Because Eastern Bluebirds forage for insects in areas where pesticides are often applied—farm fields and golf courses in particular—many are exposed either directly or indirectly, by eating contaminated insects. Birds exposed to sublethal doses become so impaired that they are easy prey for predators. Conservative estimates suggest that at least 67 million birds, including an unknown number of bluebirds, are killed by exposure to pesticides in the United States each year.

Domestic cats also represent a threat to Eastern Bluebirds, as well as most other songbirds. Investigators in Wisconsin estimate that cats kill 137 million birds per year in their state alone. Although not as vulnerable to cats as are birds that nest on the ground or regularly visit feeders, bluebirds foraging on the ground are sometimes captured and killed by cats.

Fortunately, not all human impacts have been negative. In fact, Eastern Bluebirds, more than many species of birds, have benefited from human activities. Before the arrival of Europeans in North America, the open habitats preferred by bluebirds were much less common than they are today. As a result, Eastern Bluebirds were likely found at relatively low densities throughout much of their range, primarily in the open pine and pine-oak forests of the southeastern United States and Mexico, forest openings on dry south-facing slopes and mountaintops, openings created by beaver ponds, and fire-maintained savannas. Bluebirds probably were not found in the hardwood forests of the eastern United States.

With the arrival and subsequent westward movement of Europeans, millions of acres of forests were cleared and vast open habitats created in the form of agricultural fields, pastures, and orchards. Eastern Bluebirds quickly expanded into these newly created habitats, and it's likely that Eastern Bluebird populations reached their highest levels during the late 1800s and early 1900s. Thereafter, a variety of factors, including competition from House Sparrows and European Starlings, loss of suitable habitat to urbanization and reversion of open lands to forest, and adverse weather, caused long-term declines in Eastern Bluebird populations.

Several reports on the declining bluebird populations appeared in the 1940s and 1950s. In his 1949 life history account of Eastern Bluebirds, A. C. Bent noted that "before the English sparrows came, to crowd the bluebirds out, the latter came freely to nest in the boxes that we put up for them . . . in towns and villages. So, now we must look for them in the open country, in the rural apple orchards, along the country roadsides." Over the next several years, continuing declines made it difficult to locate bluebirds even in some rural areas. In a 1959 article in *The Wilson Bulletin,* a Michigan State University ornithologist noted that observers in the state found few or no bluebirds during 1958, and on a 1,668-mile trip throughout the eastern part of the upper peninsula, they found only ten Eastern Bluebirds. Suspected causes of this decline included nest-site competitors, adverse weather, pesticide use, and loss of habitat. One investigator, referring to the use of pesticides for fire ant control in the Southeast during the late 1950s, wrote that "completion of the projected program . . . might well write the finish of this once familiar and much beloved bird."

Among the individuals who early recognized the problems faced by Eastern Bluebirds was Dr. T. E. Musselman of Quincy, Illinois, and he was also among the first to do something about it. In 1934, Musselman placed twenty-five bluebird nesting boxes along the roads of Adams County, Illinois—the first "bluebird trail." As others learned of the plight of Eastern Bluebirds during the 1950s and '60s, additional bluebird trails were established throughout the United States and Canada.

In 1966, the U.S. Fish and Wildlife Service initiated the Breeding Bird Survey to monitor breeding bird populations throughout the United States and Canada. Data collected during the first several years were encouraging, with Eastern Bluebird populations in many areas apparently stable from 1966 through the mid-1970s.

Bluebirds received additional support during the 1970s. In 1971, all three species were included on the Audubon Society's Blue List of bird species thought to be declining in numbers.

Then, in 1976, Lawrence Zeleny's *The Bluebird: How You Can Help Its Fight for Survival* was published. The book described the plight of bluebirds and explained what bluebird enthusiasts could do to help. The formation of the North American Bluebird Society in 1978 brought many of these enthusiasts together, and this organization has since played an important role in bluebird conservation.

In *The Bluebird,* Zeleny noted, "I should like to think that the recent upturn in the Eastern Bluebird population is attributable in some part at least to increased public awareness of the bluebirds' plight and the establishment of new bluebird trails and expansion of older trails." However, in what turned out to be an accurate prediction, he said that "one or two severe winters in the southern part of the country could quickly erase the recent gains."

The severe winters of the late 1970s did just that, although this crash in the bluebird population was not the first to be caused by extreme cold and snow, nor is it likely to be the last. Earlier writers noted that Eastern Bluebird populations declined dramatically after the winters of 1894–95, 1911–12, 1939–40, and 1957–58. Concerning the 1894–95 winter, one author reported that "thousands of Bluebirds perished in the storms and bitter cold which lasted for a week or more; their frozen bodies were found everywhere—in barns and other outhouses where the poor things had vainly sought shelter; in the fields and woods and even along the roadsides. To many people it was a sad spring."

Before, during, and after the severe winters of the late 1970s, an ever-growing number of "bluebirders" were responsible for erecting an increasing number of nest boxes. Thus Eastern Bluebirds that survived the winters of the late 1970s found an abundance of nest sites plus, in many areas, less competition for them. This increased availability of nest sites, in combination with a series of reasonably mild winters and, perhaps, declining populations of House Sparrows and European Starlings, has contributed to an increase in Eastern Bluebird populations throughout the United States since 1980. In fact, even including the declines of the late 1970s, the trend in Eastern Bluebird populations since 1966 has been positive in most areas.

A positive continent-wide trend does not mean that Eastern Bluebirds can now be found everywhere within their range. Attracting bluebirds to a particular location requires both suitable habitat and, at least during the breeding season, nest cavities or boxes. Other resources, including fruit, roost sites, and feeding stations, may help attract bluebirds to an area during the nonbreeding season.

In most areas, bluebirds can be readily attracted to suitable habitats by providing nest boxes. Where few or no nest sites are available, bluebirds may not be very discriminating in their choice of nest sites and may use boxes of almost any design. However, nest boxes may also attract the attention of other cavity nesters and potential predators. Careful consideration of box design and placement can maximize the chances that a box will be used by bluebirds and minimize the chances of predation.

Bluebirds readily use boxes made of wood. Cedar and red-wood are excellent choices, but other types of wood can also be used. The wood should be at least $3/4$ inch thick to provide good insulation, keeping the interior cooler during the summer and warmer during the winter. There is no need to paint or stain boxes, but if you choose to do so, use light colors that will reflect sunlight and keep the interior cooler on hot days.

The box entrance can be a round hole, vertical oval hole, or horizontal slot. The entrance should be just large enough to admit bluebirds: $1^1/2$ inches in diameter for round holes, $1^3/8$ by $2^1/4$ inches for vertical oval holes, or $1^1/8$ inches high for horizontal slots. These sizes are critical; any larger, and starlings would be able to enter the box. Bluebirds will use boxes of various depths, at times even nesting in very shallow sites, such as an apartment in a Purple Martin house. However, they are more likely to use boxes that are at least 4 inches deep from the bottom of the entrance hole to the floor and will use much deeper boxes. Boxes at least 6 inches deep may reduce the likelihood of predation, but boxes deeper than that are also preferred by potential nest-site competitors like House Sparrows. Thus in many areas, boxes 4 to 6 inches deep may be best.

Many natural cavities used by nesting bluebirds are 4 to 5 inches in diameter or even smaller, and bluebirds readily use boxes with comparable floor dimensions: 4 by 4 inches or 5 by 5 inches. Boxes with 3-by-3-inch floors will be used but may not provide sufficient room for young bluebirds. Boxes with larger floors may also be used, but bluebirds must work harder, bringing in more nest material, to produce an appropriate-size nest cup. Bluebirds given a choice of boxes selected those with 4-by-4-inch floors three times more often than those with 6-by-6-inch floors. Floor size has no apparent effect on either clutch size or nesting success. Make a few small drainage holes in the floor to allow rain to drain from the box and help keep nesting material dry.

Many bluebirders recommend the Peterson Box and the North American Bluebird Society (NABS) Box. The Peterson Box was designed, after years of studying bluebird nesting habits, by Richard Peterson of Brooklyn Center, Minnesota. Given a choice, bluebirds exhibit a preference for Peterson Boxes over other types of boxes. One reason for this preference is the unique entrance. Rather than a simple hole or slot, the entrance to a Peterson Box is $2^{1/4}$ inches high and $1^{3/8}$ inches wide, which can be made by drilling two overlapping holes with a $1^{3/8}$-inch drill bit. Bluebirds likely prefer this entrance because they can enter and exit more easily and adults can lean in to feed nestlings rather than having to enter the box to feed their young. Another advantage is that European Starlings rarely use Peterson Boxes for nesting because they prefer boxes with larger interiors.

Another important feature of the Peterson Box is the large, sloping roof, which extends well beyond the front and sides of the box. This roof makes it difficult for a mammalian predator, such as a raccoon or cat, to sit on a box and reach inside. The roof is double-layered, making the box well insulated. The unique shape of the box, which is narrower at the bottom, makes it easier for nest-building bluebirds because less nest material is needed. The box is well ventilated, and the front swings open to permit easy monitoring and cleaning.

The NABS Box is one of the boxes recommended by the North American Bluebird Society and is easier to build than the Peterson Box. It is a 4-by-4-inch rectangular box with a $1^1/2$-inch diameter entrance hole $6^1/2$ inches from the bottom of the box and a sloping roof. One side swings open to permit monitoring and cleaning. Instructions for building the NABS Box and other boxes can be obtained from the North American Bluebird Society, Department B, P.O. Box 74, Darlington, WI 53530-0074 (or on the society's website: www.nabluebirdsociety.org).

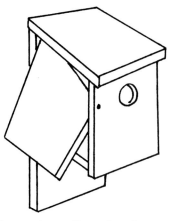

Adding a piece of wood at the entrance of a box to make a tunnel-like opening may make it more difficult for predators like cats or raccoons to reach a bluebird nest. Such predator guards are not always effective, however, especially with raccoons, and if the total length of the entrance hole is too long—more than about $1^1/2$ inches—it may deter bluebirds from using the box.

A predator guard made of hardware cloth is more effective at deterring predators. Such guards may make the box less attractive to bluebirds, and some bluebirders recommend that the guard not be attached until after bluebirds have completed nest construction and started egg laying. Others have found that leaving these guards on year-round does not deter bluebirds from using a box.

Bluebird boxes should be placed in open areas with low or sparse ground cover and a few trees, shrubs, or utility wires to serve as perch sites. Suitable areas include, but are not limited to, pastures, hayfields, old fields, large rural lawns, orchards, cemeteries, roadsides, golf courses (unless pesticides are used on a regular basis), and open woodlots. To minimize competition with House Sparrows, boxes should be placed at least 200 yards from farms, feedlots, or any other areas these birds frequent. House Wrens are also nest-site competitors, but because wrens prefer to nest in forest and forest edge habitat, competition can be minimized by placing boxes in more open areas at least 100 feet from the nearest forest edge. Boxes so placed are also less likely to attract predators such as raccoons and snakes.

Yet another species that sometimes uses nest boxes meant for bluebirds is the Tree Swallow. Although many nest near water, Tree Swallows frequently nest in the same open habitats occupied by bluebirds, and they will readily use any box that a bluebird would use. One solution to this problem is to provide a pair of boxes—one for bluebirds and one for Tree Swallows. These boxes should be 5 to 25 feet apart; if they are any farther apart, Tree Swallows, which defend only a small area around their nest sites, may use both.

Some open areas may just be large enough for a single pair of bluebirds, and in such areas, a single box may attract a breeding pair. Putting up two boxes may make an area even more attractive to bluebirds, however. Where there are larger expanses of blue-bird habitat, a series, or trail, of boxes—or even better, a series of paired boxes—can be provided. Here, boxes or pairs of boxes should be placed at least 300 feet apart.

Most bluebirders recommend that boxes be placed 4 to 6 feet above the ground, although Eastern Bluebirds will nest in boxes ranging from 2 to 20 feet high. Very low boxes are more vulnerable to climbing or jumping predators, such as cats, and very high boxes may be more attractive to House Sparrows and are more difficult to access for maintenance and cleaning.

Boxes can be mounted on trees, fence posts, utility poles, or other posts or pipes. Boxes on trees would seem to best approximate a natural cavity nest site, and bluebirds certainly can nest successfully in tree-mounted boxes. But nest predation is often a problem in these boxes, because trees are so easily climbed by raccoons, cats, snakes, and other potential preda-tors. Boxes on trees are also more likely to be damaged or otherwise disturbed by squirrels, which often chew on and enlarge the entrances, possibly making the boxes accessible to Euro-pean Starlings.

Studies in some areas have found that bluebirds are more likely to use boxes mounted on posts or utility poles than those mounted on trees. Before using a utility pole, get permission from the telephone or power company. One disadvantage of mounting boxes on utility poles near roads is that some bluebirds nesting along roads, especially those with a lot of traffic, are killed. If the utility pole is near a road, orient the box away from the road to reduce the chances that bluebirds will be hit by passing vehicles.

In areas with few raccoons, fence posts are good places to mount bluebird boxes (but if they are not on your property, first get permission from the landowner). The best place to mount a bluebird box, however, may be at or near the top of a smooth, clean pipe or pole. One important advantage is that the bluebird box can be placed where bluebirds are most likely to use it and nest successfully. Three-quarter-inch EMT (electrical metallic tubing) conduit pipe works particularly well because its slick zinc-plated surface is difficult for predators to climb. Other types and diameters of round pipes or poles also work well. The pipe or pole should be at least 6 or 7 feet long—sufficient to mount the box 4 or 5 feet high and drive the pipe or pole about 2 feet into the ground to keep the box stable. Mount the box by drilling two holes through the pipe or pole and the back of the box, then using bolts to anchor the box in place. To further deter pole-climbing predators, apply car wax, silicone spray, or automotive grease to the pipe or pole.

Boxes can be put up at any time. To attract a breeding pair, the box needs to be in place before the start of the bluebird breeding season. Resident bluebirds may locate and even begin to defend nest boxes well before the start of breeding season, so boxes put up in the fall or early winter may have a better chance of being used by bluebirds during the next breeding season. In addition, these boxes may be used by roosting bluebirds during long, cold winter nights. Boxes can be temporarily winterized by plugging ventilation holes and generally making them as airtight as possible. This helps keep the interior warmer and can save a roosting bluebird valuable energy.

After bluebird boxes are in place, you should monitor them. House Sparrow nests—which usually fill the box and consist of dry grass, feathers, and occasionally, plastic—should be removed immediately. Do not open boxes with nesting bluebirds after nestlings are twelve to fourteen days old. Disturbances may cause nestlings this age to fledge prematurely, and their chances of survival will be much reduced. After young bluebirds have fledged, the old nest can be removed. Even if it's not removed, however, bluebirds may renest in the same box. In fact, a recent Kentucky study showed that bluebirds, given a choice, preferred boxes with old nests. Nevertheless, old nest material must eventually be removed; after repeated reuse, and the addition of new nest material with each nesting attempt, nest material will accumulate to the point that the box is too shallow and will not be used by bluebirds.

Continued monitoring of your nest box will help ensure that they are used only by bluebirds and native species like Tree Swallows or House Wrens. The information you gather can help researchers learn more about which species use which boxes, how many eggs are laid, when eggs hatch, and when the young birds fledge. To share your information and become part of a continent-wide effort to learn more about bluebirds, contact the North American Bluebird Society or the Cornell Laboratory of Ornithology (birdsource.cornell.edu/birdhouse/index.html).

Planting trees, shrubs, and vines that provide fruit and shelter will also aid and attract bluebirds. As an added bonus, the presence of fruit will also attract a variety of other birds, including Cedar Waxwings, American Robins, Baltimore Orioles, Northern Mockingbirds, and Gray Catbirds. From late summer through early spring, fruit may be an important part of a bluebird's diet, and during periods of cold weather when insects are not available, it may be essential. Eastern Bluebirds will consume a wide variety of fruits, and providing several different types of plants that bear fruit at different times will help ensure a longer-lasting supply. Appropriate plant species vary with location; choose those that grow well in your area.

Because they feed on insects and fruit rather than seeds, bluebirds do not come to feeders as readily as many other species of birds. The key is getting bluebirds to recognize a feeding station as a place to obtain food. Initially, the feeder should be placed where bluebirds can see it, and providing live, moving food such as mealworms, grubs, and waxworms may attract their attention. Once bluebirds start visiting a feeder, it can be gradually moved to another location.

In addition to live prey, bluebirds visiting a feeding station will eat suet, currants, raisins soaked briefly in boiling water to soften them, and wild fruits and berries, which can be harvested, then frozen or dehydrated for later use as bluebird food. A variety of bluebird food mixes are commercially available, containing such things as suet, corn flour, dried insects, and raisins.

Linda Peterson Janilla of Minnesota has developed a mixture that she has found to be readily consumed by bluebirds. To make this mixture, which she calls Bluebird Banquet, mix 1 cup peanut butter, 4 cups yellow cornmeal, and 1 cup unbleached or whole-wheat flour. Add 1 cup fine sunflower seed chips, 1 cup peanut hearts or finely ground nuts, and $^{1}/_{2}$ to 1 cup Zante currants or halved raisins. Drizzle and stir in 1 cup rendered, melted suet, available commercially as pure suet cakes. Allow the mixture to cool. The resulting mix will be crumbly and should have pea-size lumps. If too sticky after cooling, mix in a little more flour; if too dry, drizzle in more melted suet. Refrigerate the mixture until fed to bluebirds.

Feeding stations may be visited by bluebirds more often during cold weather, when insects may not be available. Providing food for bluebirds during the winter and early spring, when they may be arriving at northern breeding areas, may increase their chances of surviving periods of inclement weather.

In drier areas or during prolonged dry periods, and during extended periods of subfreezing temperatures, water can become a scarce resource. Bluebirds get some water from their food but always require access to water for drinking and bathing. Water can be provided in a number of ways, from an upside-down garbage can lid to a birdbath to an inground pond. Whatever you use to hold the water, it should provide a gradual incline into the water and must always be kept filled.

Providing bluebirds with needed resources not only gives you excellent opportunities to closely observe these beautiful and fascinating birds, but also aids in bluebird conservation. As Lawrence Zeleny pointed out in *The Bluebird,* people who are truly concerned about our wildlife heritage long for an opportunity to do something tangible and to become personally involved. Bluebird conservation provides this opportunity, and the results of your efforts will soon be apparent.

References

Allaire, P. N. 1976. Nesting adaptations of bluebirds on surface-mined lands. *Kentucky Warbler* 52:70–72.

Allen, D. H. 1988. Home range and habitat use of Eastern Bluebirds on the Savannah River Plant, South Carolina. M.S. thesis, Clemson Univ., Clemson, SC.

Andrews, R. W., and C. E. Bock. 1979. A Christmas Bird Count analysis of bluebird abundance patterns and population trends. *Sialia* 1:10–14.

Avise, J. C., J. C. Patton, and C. F. Aquadro. 1980. Evolutionary genetics of birds. I. Relationships among North American thrushes and allies. *Auk* 97:135–47.

Beal, F. 1915. Food of the robins and bluebirds of the United States. *Bull. U.S. Dept. Agriculture* 171:1–31.

Belser, C. G. 1981. Seasonal ethograms of the Eastern Bluebird near Clemson, South Carolina. M.S. thesis, Clemson Univ., Clemson, SC.

Bent, A. C. 1949. Life histories of North American thrushes, kinglets, and their allies. *U.S. Natl. Mus. Bull.* 196.

Butler, A. W. 1898. *The birds of Indiana.* Annual Report, Indiana Dept. of Geology and Natural Resources.

Conner, R. N., and C. S. Adkisson. 1974. Eastern Bluebirds nesting in clearcuts. *J. Wildl. Manage.* 38:934–35.

Davis, W. H. 1997. That remarkable Peterson entrance. *Sialia* 19:48–49.

Davis, W. H., P. J. Kalisz, and R. J. Wells. 1994. Eastern Bluebirds prefer boxes containing old nests. *J. Field Ornithol.* 65:250–53.

Davis, W. H., and W. C. McComb. 1988. Use of tangle trap to measure snake predation at bluebird boxes. *Sialia* 10:87–88.

Davis, W. H., and P. Roca. 1995. *Bluebirds and their survival.* Univ. Press of Kentucky, Lexington.

Droge, D. L., P. A. Gowaty, and W. W. Weathers. 1991. Sex-biased provisioning: a test for differences in field metabolic rates of nestling Eastern Bluebirds. *Condor* 93:793–98.

Dunn, J. 1981. The identification of female bluebirds. *Birding* 13:4–11.

Fiedler, D. A. 1974. The ecology of the Eastern Bluebird in central Minnesota. M.A. thesis, St. Cloud State College, St. Cloud, MN.

Finch, J. R. 1987. Is there a need to feed bluebirds? *Sialia* 9:11–14.

Flanigan, A. B. 1971. Predation on snakes by Eastern Bluebird and Brown Thrasher. *Wilson Bull.* 83:441.

Frazier, A., and V. Nolan. 1959. Communal roosting by the Eastern Bluebird in winter. *Bird-Banding* 30:219–26.

Goldman, P. 1975. Hunting behavior of Eastern Bluebirds. *Auk* 92:798–801.

Gowaty, P. A. 1980. The origin of mating system variability and behavioral and demographic correlates of the mating system in Eastern Bluebirds. Ph.D. diss., Clemson Univ., Clemson, SC.

Gowaty, P. A. 1981. Aggression of breeding Eastern Bluebirds toward their mates and models of intra- and interspecific intruders. *Anim. Behav.* 29:1013–27.

Gowaty, P. A. 1983. Male parental care and apparent monogamy among Eastern Bluebirds. *Am. Nat.* 121:149–57.

Gowaty, P. A. 1984. House Sparrows kill Eastern Bluebirds. *J. Field Ornithol.* 55:378–80.

Gowaty, P. A. 1991. Facultative manipulation of sex ratios in birds: rare or rarely observed? *Curr. Ornithol.* 8:141–71.

Gowaty, P. A., and W. C. Bridges. 1991. Behavioral, demographic, and environmental correlates of extra-pair fertilizations in Eastern Bluebirds. *Behav. Ecol.* 2:339–50.

Gowaty, P. A., and W. C. Bridges. 1991. Nestbox availability affects extra-pair fertilizations and conspecific nest parasitism in Eastern Bluebirds. *Anim. Behav.* 41:661–75.

Gowaty, P. A., and J. H. Plissner. 1997. Breeding dispersal of Eastern Bluebirds depends on nesting success but not on removal of old nests: an experimental study. *J. Field Ornithol.* 68:323–30.

Gowaty, P. A., and J. H. Plissner. 1998. Eastern Bluebird. In: *The Birds of North America,* No. 381 (A. Poole and F. Gill, eds.). The Birds of North America, Inc., Philadelphia, PA.

Gowaty, P. A., and S. J. Wagner. 1988. Breeding season aggression of female and male Eastern Bluebirds to models of potential conspecific and interspecific egg dumpers. *Ethology* 78:238–50.

Gowaty, P. A., J. H. Plissner, and T. G. Williams. 1989. Behavioural correlates of uncertain parentage: mate guarding and nest guarding by Eastern Bluebirds. *Anim. Behav.* 38:272–84.

Gower, C. 1936. The cause of blue color as found in the bluebird and the blue jay. *Auk* 53:178–85.

Hartshorne, J. M. 1962. Behavior of the Eastern Bluebird at the nest. *Living Bird* 1:131–49.

Hensley, R. C., and K. G. Smith. 1986. Eastern Bluebird responses to nocturnal black rat snake nest predation. *Wilson Bull.* 98:602–3.

Hill, G. E. 1994. Geographic variation in male ornamentation and female mate preference in the House Finch: a comparative test of models of sexual selection. *Behav. Ecol.* 5:64–73.

Horn, D. J., M. Benninger-Truax, and D. W. Ulaszewski. 1996. The influence of habitat characteristics on nestbox selection by Eastern Bluebirds and four competitors. *Ohio J. Sci.* 96:57–59.

Huntsman, B. O. 1995. The functions of singing by male Eastern Bluebirds. M.S. thesis, Eastern Kentucky Univ., Richmond, KY.

James, D. A., and J. C. Neal. 1986. Arkansas birds: their distribution and abundance. Univ. of Arkansas Press, Fayetteville, AR.

Kaufman, K. 1992. The practiced eye: bluebirds. *Am. Birds* 46:159–62.

Kerr, R. A. 1985. Wild string of winters confirmed. *Science* 227:506.

Keyser, A. J. 1998. Is structural color a reliable signal of quality in Blue Grosbeaks? M.S. thesis, Auburn Univ., Auburn, AL.

Krieg, D. C. 1971. *The behavioral patterns of the Eastern Bluebird.* New York State Museum and Science Service, Bull. No. 415. Albany, NY.

Kruger, S. M. 1985. Productivity and nest-site selection of Eastern Bluebirds in Wisconsin. M.S. thesis, Univ. of Wisconsin, Stevens Point, WI.

Laskey, A. R. 1939. A study of nesting Eastern Bluebirds. *Bird-Banding* 10:23–32.

Ligon, J. D. 1969. Factors influencing breeding range expansion of the Azure Bluebird. *Wilson Bull.* 81:104–5.

Lombardo, M. P. 1982. Sex ratios in the Eastern Bluebird. *Evolution* 36:615–17.

MacDougall-Shackleton, E. A., and R. J. Robertson. 1998. Confidence of paternity and paternal care by Eastern Bluebirds. *Behav. Ecol.* 9:201–5.

McComb, W. C., W. H. Davis, and P. N. Allaire. 1987. Excluding starlings from a slot entrance bluebird nest box. *Wildl. Soc. Bull.* 15:204–7.

Meek, S. B., and R. J. Robertson. 1991. Adoption of young by replacement male birds: an experimental study of Eastern Bluebirds and a review. *Anim. Behav.* 42:813–20.

Meek, S. B., and R. J. Robertson. 1992. How do floater male Eastern Bluebirds benefit by filling vacancies on territories where females already have young? *Behav. Ecol.* 3:95–101.

Meek, S. B., and R. J. Robertson. 1994. Interspecific competition for nestboxes affects mate guarding in Eastern Bluebirds. *Anim. Behav.* 47:295–302.

Meek, S. B., and R. J. Robertson. 1994. Time of day of egg laying by Eastern Bluebirds. *Wilson Bull.* 107:377–79.

Meek, S. B., R. J. Robertson, and P. T. Boag. 1994. Extrapair paternity and intraspecific brood parasitism in Eastern Bluebirds revealed by DNA fingerprinting. *Auk* 111:739–44.

Otello, D. B. 1982. Habitat structure around nests of Eastern Bluebirds. M.S. thesis, Univ. of Massachusetts, Amherst, MA.

Palokangas, P., E. Korpimaki, H. Hakkarainen, E. Huhta, P. Tolonen, and R. V. Alatalo. 1994. Female kestrels gain reproductive success by choosing brightly ornamented males. *Anim. Behav.* 47:443–48.

Peakall, D. B. 1970. The Eastern Bluebird: its breeding season, clutch size, and nesting success. *Living Bird* 9:239–56.

Pierson, T. A., and P. F. Scanlon. 1986. Use of fencepost cavities by nesting Eastern Bluebirds in southwestern Virginia. *Wilson Bull.* 98:479–82.

Pinkowski, B. C. 1971. Some observations on the vocalizations of the Eastern Bluebird. *Bird-Banding* 42:20–27.

Pinkowski, B. C. 1971. An analysis of banding recovery data on Eastern Bluebirds in Michigan and three neighboring states. *Jack-Pine Warbler* 49:33–50.

Pinkowski, B. C. 1974. A comparative study of the behavioral and breeding ecology of the Eastern Bluebird. Ph.D. diss., Wayne State Univ., Detroit, MI.

Pinkowski, B. C. 1974. The Eastern Bluebird pair bond: comments and calculations. *Inland Bird Banding News* 37:107–10.

Pinkowski, B. C. 1975. Growth and development of Eastern Bluebirds. *Bird-Banding* 46:273–89.

Pinkowski, B. C. 1976. Photoperiodic effects on the postjuvenal molt of the Eastern Bluebird. *Ohio J. Sci.* 76:268–73.

Pinkowski, B. C. 1977. Breeding adaptations in the Eastern Bluebird. *Condor* 79:289–302.

Pinkowski, B. C. 1977. Foraging behavior of the Eastern Bluebird. *Wilson Bull.* 89:404–14.

Pinkowski, B. C. 1978. Feeding of nestling and fledgling Eastern Bluebirds. *Wilson Bull.* 90:84–98.

Pinkowski, B. C. 1979. Annual productivity and its measurement in a multi-brooded passerine, the Eastern Bluebird. *Auk* 96:562–72.

Pinkowski, B. C. 1979. Tremble-thrusts. *Sialia* 1:112–13.

Pinkowski, B. C. 1979. Effects of a severe winter on a breeding population of Eastern Bluebirds. *Jack-Pine Warbler* 57:9–12.

Pinkowski, B. C. 1979. Nest site selection in Eastern Bluebirds. *Condor* 81:435–36.

Pinkowski, B. C. 1979. Time budget and incubation rhythm of the Eastern Bluebird. *Am. Midl. Nat.* 101:427–33.

Pitts, T. D. 1976. Nesting habits of Eastern Bluebirds in northwest Tennessee. Ph.D. diss., Univ. of Tennessee, Knoxville, TN.

Pitts, T. D. 1978. Eastern Bluebird mortality at winter roosts in Tennessee. *Bird-Banding* 49:77–78.

Pitts, T. D. 1978. Foods of Eastern Bluebird nestlings in northwest Tennessee. *J. Tenn. Acad. Sci.* 53:136–39.

Pitts, T. D. 1979. Foods of Eastern Bluebirds during exceptionally cold weather in Tennessee. *J. Wildl. Manage.* 43:752–54.

Pitts, T. D. 1981. Eastern Bluebird population fluctuations in Tennessee during 1970–1979. *Migrant* 52:29–37.

Pitts, T. D. 1985. Identification of second-year and after-second-year Eastern Bluebirds. *J. Field Ornithol.* 56:422–24.

Pitts, T. D. 1988. Effects of nest box size on Eastern Bluebird nests. *J. Field Ornithol.* 59:309–13.

Pitts, T. D., M. Conner, S. Crews, M. Crutcher, J. Hobbs, J. King, J. Martin, T. Martin, T. McCraw, J. Rayfield, and J. Wray. 1989. Winter plant foods of Eastern Bluebirds in Tennessee. *Sialia* 11:57–61.

Pitts, T. D., and R. W. Snow. 1996. Mortality of banded adult Eastern Bluebirds. *Sialia* 18:83–93.

Plissner, J. H., and P. A. Gowaty. 1988. Evidence of reproductive error in adoption of nestling Eastern Bluebirds. *Auk* 105:575–78.

Plissner, J. H., and P. A. Gowaty. 1995. Eastern Bluebirds are attracted to two-box sites. *Wilson Bull.* 107:289–97.

Plissner, J. H., and P. A. Gowaty. 1996. Patterns of natal dispersal, turnover, and dispersal costs in Eastern Bluebirds. *Anim. Behav.* 51:1307–22.

Preston, F. W., and J. McCormick. 1948. The eyesight of the bluebird. *Wilson Bull.* 60:120–21.

Price, J., S. Droege, and A. Price. 1995. *The summer atlas of North American birds.* Academic Press, London.

Roby, D. D., K. L. Brink, and K. Wittmann. 1992. Effects of bird blowfly parasitism on Eastern Bluebird and Tree Swallow nestlings. *Wilson Bull.* 104:630–43.

Root, T. 1988. *Atlas of wintering North American birds: an analysis of Christmas Bird Count data.* Univ. of Chicago Press, Chicago, IL.

Rounds, R. C., and H. L. Munro. 1982. A review of hybridization between *Sialia sialis* and *S. currucoides. Wilson Bull.* 94:219–23.

Sauer, J. R., and S. Droege. 1990. Recent population trends of the Eastern Bluebird. *Wilson Bull.* 102:239–52.

Savereno, A. J. 1991. Seasonal home ranges of and habitat use by Eastern Bluebirds. M.S. thesis, Clemson Univ., Clemson, SC.

Scriven, D. H. 1993. *Bluebird trails: a guide to success.* Bluebird Recovery Committee of the Audubon Chapter of Minneapolis, Minneapolis, MN.

Scriven, D. H. 1998. The Peterson bluebird nest box. *Sialia* 20:103.

Stevenson, H. M., and B. H. Anderson. 1994. *The birdlife of Florida.* Univ. Presses of Florida, Gainesville, FL.

Stokes, D. W., and L. Q. Stokes. 1989. Eastern Bluebird, pp. 313–25. In: *A guide to bird behavior,* vol. III. Little, Brown and Co., New York.

Stokes, D. W., and L. Q. Stokes. 1991. *The Bluebird Book: The Complete Guide to Attracting Bluebirds.* Little, Brown, and Co., New York.

Thomas, R. H. 1946. A study of Eastern Bluebirds in Arkansas. *Wilson Bull.* 58:143–83.

Wallace, G. J. 1959. The plight of the bluebird in Michigan. *Wilson Bull.* 71:192–93.

Webster, J. D. 1973. Middle American races of the Eastern Bluebird. *Auk* 90:579–90.

Wittman, K., and R. C. Beason. 1992. The effect of blowfly parasitism on nestling Eastern Bluebird development. *J. Field Ornithol.* 63:286–93.

Woodward, P. W., and J. C. Woodward. 1979. Brown-headed Cowbird parasitism on Eastern Bluebirds. *Wilson Bull.* 91:321–22.

Zeleny, L. 1976. *The Bluebird: How You Can Help Its Fight for Survival.* Indiana Univ. Press, Bloomington, IN.

Zeleny, L. 1986. What happens when a parent bluebird dies? *Sialia* 8:103–5.

Photo Credits

Page 1
Bill Marchel

Page 2
Ron Austing (top)
Bill Marchel (bottom)

Page 3
Robert McCaw

Page 4
D. Dvorak Jr. (top)
Connie Toops (bottom)

Page 5
Richard Day/Daybreak Imagery
(top)
Connie Toops (bottom)

Page 6
Tom Vezo (top)
Ron Austing (bottom)

Page 7
Doug Locke

Page 8
Robert McCaw (top)
D. Dvorak Jr. (bottom)

Page 9
Robert McCaw

Page 10
Gary Carter

Page 11
Robert McCaw

Page 13
Robert McCaw (top)
Connie Toops (bottom)

Page 14
Robert McCaw

Page 15
Jim Flynn

Page 16
Gregory K. Scott

Page 17
Tom Vezo (top)
Maslowski Photo (bottom)

Page 18
Tom Vezo (top)
Richard Day/Daybreak Imagery
(bottom)

Page 19
Bill Marchel

Page 20
Maslowski Photo

Page 21
Ron Austing (top)
Doug Locke (bottom)

Page 22
Robert McCaw

Page 23
Robert McCaw

Page 24
Heather R. Davidson

Page 25
Tom Vezo (top)
Connie Toops (bottom)

Page 26
Bill Marchel

Page 27
D. Dvorak Jr. (top)
Doug Locke (bottom)

Page 28
J. R. McTammany (top)
D. Dvorak Jr. (bottom)

Page 29
Bill Leaman

Page 31
Robert McCaw

Page 32
Doug Locke

Page 33
Ron Austing

Page 34
Robert McCaw

Page 35
Steve Maslowski

Page 36
Richard Day/Daybreak Imagery
(left)
Bill Marchel (right)

Page 37
D. Dvorak Jr.

Page 38
Connie Toops (top)
Richard Day/Daybreak Imagery
(bottom)

Page 39
Gregory K. Scott (top)
Cliff Beittel (bottom)

Page 40
Bill Marchel

Page 41
Robert McCaw

Page 42
Bill Leaman

Page 43
Robert McCaw (top)
Connie Toops (bottom)

Page 44
Robert McCaw

Page 45
Cliff Beittel

Page 46
Maslowski Photo

Page 47
Ron Austing (top)
Steve and Dave Maslowski
(bottom)

Page 48
Wayne Lynch (top)
Gregory K. Scott (bottom)

Page 49
Maslowski Photo (top)
Robert McCaw (bottom)

Page 50
Connie Toops

Page 51
Connie Toops

Page 52
Ron Austing (top)
Bill Marchel (bottom)

Page 53
Bill Marchel

Page 54
Leonard Lee Rue III (top)
Ron Austing (bottom)

Page 55
Richard Day/Daybreak Imagery

Page 56
Ron Austing

Page 57
Bill Marchel

Page 58
Richard Day/Daybreak Imagery
(top)
Bill Marchel (bottom)

Page 59
Leonard Lee Rue III

Page 60
Robert McCaw

Page 61
Robert McCaw

Page 62
Maslowski Photo (top)
Connie Toops (bottom)

Page 63
Ron Austing

Page 64
Robert McCaw

Page 65
Steve Maslowski (top)
Bill Duyck (bottom)

Page 66
Ron Austing

Page 67
Ron Austing

Page 68
Bill Duyck

Page 69
Tom Vezo

Page 70
Ron Austing

Page 71
Doug Locke

Page 72
Bill Duyck (top)
Russell C. Hansen (bottom)

Page 73
Bill Duyck (top)
Maslowski Photo (bottom)

Page 74
Gary Carter

Page 75
Bill Duyck

Page 76
Russell C. Hansen (top)
J. R. McTammany (bottom)

Page 77
Bill Duyck

Page 78
Leonard Lee Rue III (top)
Gary W. Carter (bottom)

Page 79
J. R. McTammany

Page 80
Russell C. Hansen (top)
D. Dvorak Jr. (bottom)

Page 81
Gregory K. Scott

Page 82
Maslowski Photo

Page 83
Gregory K. Scott

Page 84
Gregory K. Scott

Page 85
Ron Austing (top)
Todd Fink/Daybreak Imagery
(bottom)

Page 86
Steve Maslowski (top)
D. Dvorak Jr. (bottom)

Page 87
Heather R. Davidson

Page 89
Bill Leaman

Page 90
Richard Day/Daybreak Imagery

Page 91
Richard Day/Daybreak Imagery

Page 92
D. Dvorak Jr. (top)
Russell C. Hansen (bottom)

Page 93
Connie Toops

Page 94
D. Dvorak Jr.

Page 95
Maslowski Photo (top)
D. Dvorak Jr. (bottom)

Page 96
Jim Flynn

Page 97
Robert McCaw

Page 98
Robert McCaw

Page 99
Heather R. Davidson

Page 100
Doug Locke (top)
Gary W. Carter (bottom)

Page 101
Gary W. Carter (top)
Jim Flynn (bottom)

Page 102
D. Dvorak Jr. (top)
Richard Day/Daybreak Imagery
(bottom)

Page 103
Doug Locke (top)
Susan Day/Daybreak Imagery
(bottom)

Page 104
Richard Day/Daybreak Imagery

Page 105
Leonard Lee Rue III

Page 106
Richard Day/Daybreak Imagery

Page 107
Richard Day/Daybreak Imagery

Page 108
Gregory K. Scott (top)
Doug Locke (bottom)

About the Author

Gary Ritchison is a professor of biological sciences at Eastern Kentucky University. He has published in numerous ornithological journals and presented papers on the behavior and ecology of birds to several academic societies. He is the author of Stackpole's Wild Bird Guides *Northern Cardinal* and *Downy Woodpecker* and lives in Richmond, Kentucky.